An

OCKLAWAHA RIVER ODYSSEY

PADDLING THROUGH NATURAL HISTORY

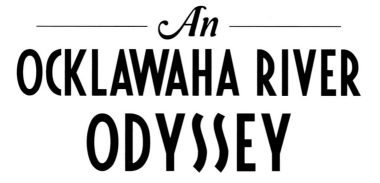

ELIZABETH RANDALL

· ·

PHOTOGRAPHS BY **BOB RANDALL**
FOREWORD BY **BOB H. LEE**

THE
History
PRESS

Published by The History Press
Charleston, SC
www.historypress.net

Front cover, top (left to right): Davenport Landing; tiny turtle on Silver River; our red tandem kayak we used to travel from Gores Landing to the Ocklawaha Outpost; *bottom (and opposite page)*: Great blue heron at sunrise on Silver River.

Back cover (clockwise from top left): Crossing Rodman Reservoir; belted kingfisher on the Ocklawaha River; the front of Rodman dam.

First published 2019

Manufactured in the United States

ISBN 9781467139632

Library of Congress Control Number: 2019939736

For the next generation, especially Jamison, Evelyn and Jesse.

Hope and the future for me are not in lawns and cultivated fields, not in towns and cities, but in the impervious and quaking swamps.
—Henry David Thoreau, "The Swamp Lover"

Nature holds the key to our aesthetic, intellectual, cognitive and even spiritual satisfaction.
—E.O. Wilson

CONTENTS

CONTENTS

FOREWORD

My initiation into the joys of the Ocklawaha River comes from an intimacy most folks would *never* want to experience. The year was 1978, when I was a rookie game warden on water patrol, at night, alone, and without backup in the jungle environs of the Ocklawaha. By midnight, I heard a faint trickle that quickly became a flood that led to me being summarily immersed in the creek's tepid waters while I watched my patrol boat disappear, stern first, in a release of gaseous bubbles. I was left astraddle a six-gallon gas can floating through a gauntlet of alligators. I affectionately label this story "Midnight Ride on a Six-Gallon Gas Can" in my first book, *Backcountry Lawman*. And it was this book that led to a friendship with Liz Randall and her husband, Bob.

Liz and I were scheduled lecturers at the 2017 Florida Heritage Book Festival in St. Augustine. My talk was relegated to a small classroom; Liz was given an entire auditorium—and rightly so. She was introducing her recently published book, *Murder in St. Augustine: The Mysterious Death of Athalia Ponsell Lindsley*. I snuck in at the last moment and was lucky to find a seat amongst a packed house. What struck an emotional chord with me was how eerily similar her father's unsolved murder was to that of Athalia.

Athalia's killer was never arrested, but Liz ably put forth a point-by-point argument, augmented with 1970s black-and-white crime scene photos, about who hacked poor Athalia down with a machete in broad daylight.

After Liz's talk, I introduced myself, met Bob, and asked her to sign my copy of her book. One thing led to another, and before I knew it, Liz told me of her next project. Brimming with enthusiasm, she explained how she would write about the Ocklawaha River.

"Think of it as kind of a paddling travelogue with a good dose of local history and lore included." Her eyes began to sparkle, then she added, "And that's where you come in. Please take Bob and me on a boat ride down the Ocklawaha."

Few people can refuse the offer to opine on one of their favorite subjects. I told Liz and Bob that of course, I would be delighted to take them on a tour. The part I was intimately familiar with and had patrolled so often in the past was a ten-mile strip downstream from Rodman Dam to its confluence with the St. Johns River. Rather than kayak it, we would take a powerboat. Yes, I knew this violated the true spirit of manual propulsion and the principles of everything "green," but it would be a more efficient method of travel, as there was much I wanted to show them. This would also turn out to be the last leg in their journey.

Liz Randall is a high school English teacher, published freelance writer and the author of five nonfiction books. Being one of the first who was privileged to read *An Ocklawaha River Odyssey*, I was struck with how artfully she blended her and Bob's personal exploration of the Ocklawaha by kayak—beginning at Silver Springs and ending at the St. Johns River—with her research into the river's rich and colorful history, including what it was like before the middle river was destroyed to dig the ill-fated Cross-Florida Barge Canal. Included is a poignant passage from my good friend, Donnie Adams, in which he describes his last journey on the pristine Ocklawaha before the forest floodplain was destroyed and Rodman Dam was constructed. To provide added context to this contentious issue, Liz explores the pros and cons of breaching Rodman Dam and restoring the Ocklawaha to the free-flowing river it once was. You will also learn of the steamboat paddle wheelers and the Hubbard Hart Line and how Hart first brought tourism to the interior of northeast Florida.

In a later chapter, she tells of her and Bob's hands-on tutelage in electrofishing by a Florida Fish and Wildlife Conservation Commission biologist. In my experience, it's the biologists who really know what a fishery is like for any given body of water (as opposed to the anecdotal evidence presented by sport fishermen).

Experienced and aspiring paddlers will come away with a detailed understanding of where to go, who to contact and how far they will be paddling should they want to replicate all or part of Liz and Bob's amazing journey.

So, I invite you to join the Randalls in an armchair waterway adventure, to dip your vicarious paddle and watch the shore drift by. It'll be great fun.

BOB H. LEE
August 11, 2018

OCKLAWAHA RIVER OYDSSEY

December 1, 2017

> *It is grand, impressive, strangely tropical—now fairylike and charming,*
> *and again, weird and wild.*
> —*Frances DeVore*

It had been almost a year since my husband and I first pushed off in a friend's canoe to discover the Ocklawaha River. Now, we were in Silver Springs State Park, a popular tourist spot in Ocala, Florida, ready to embark on a five-day, forty-five-mile camping and paddling trip with twenty-four kayaking enthusiasts on a downstream paddle on the Ocklawaha River. We would all leave our cars at the launch point, Silver Springs State Park, for the duration of the trip. At the trip's conclusion, paddlers and their boats and gear would be shuttled back to Silver Springs from the Rodman Reservoir, the huge, fifteen-mile-long impoundment on the Ocklawaha River west of Palatka.

Bob and I had paddled, or rode as passengers, on most of the Ocklawaha River already on the numerous day trips documented in part one of this book. Now, for part two, we would paddle most of the lower river and regain miles lost here and there. We were ready—Bob even had a map of the river sectioned into pages and sheathed in plastic sleeves, with the Lost Springs highlighted in green. It seemed all our previous experiences coalesced for this particular trip. We knew what to do and how and where to go about doing it.

We had rented a tandem kayak from the Ocklawaha Canoe Outpost and brought our tent and sleeping bags. Paddle Florida—the 501 nonprofit organization dedicated to promoting water conservation, wildlife preservation, springs restoration and waterways protection across Florida—was hosting the event. Paddle Florida would feed us and transport our gear from place to place. We would sleep in a tent outdoors by the side of the river and, for one night, in a prefab cabin at the Ocklawaha Outpost (a goal of mine since the previous winter).

We asked ourselves: What would we find? What would be different? What would be the same?

How had Bob, an air force brat who once lived in Turkey, and I, a former city girl from New York, gotten here in the first place?

Part of the reason was a break from our last book, a true-crime treatise, which sent us hurtling back to the soothing balm of backwoods nature. Another reason was this: We'd lived in Florida for close to half a century. People fly here from all over the world to experience its natural beauty. If there was treasure in our own backyard, we wanted to experience it.

First, we had to find it. And find it we did, in fumbling, naive and inexperienced ways. Steadier hands, experienced voices and knowledgeable insights helped us along on our adventure.

Here is how we did it…

ACKNOWLEDGEMENTS

Many people contributed their valuable information, expertise, and perspective for this book. Thanks to Lisa Rinaman, the St. Johns Riverkeeper; Larry Beaton, steamboat historian; Mike Stallings, archeologist; Bobby Parker, Matheson Museum; Craig Lindauer, park services specialist for Silver Springs State Park; Jim Gross, executive director of the Florida Defenders of the Environment; Captain Erika Ritter, A Cruising Down the River; Paul Nosca, "Ocklawahaman"; Captain Karen Chadwick, navigator and historian; Elizabeth Howard, granddaughter of steamboat captain James Hatton Howard II; Greg Barton, Florida Forest Service; Matt Keene, filmmaker; Margaret Ross Tolbert, artist; Donnie Adams, master builder, historian and artist; Lisa Dunbar, senior museum curator, Museum of Florida History; and Bill Richards and Janice Hindson of Paddle Florida. Title credit goes to Jill Lingard of Paddle Florida. Special thanks to mentors Bob H. Lee, esteemed author and retired game warden, and Jack Bass, the last true Floridian. Any mistakes in this account are strictly my own.

INTRODUCTION

This is the forest primeval. The murmuring pines and the hemlocks…
—Henry Wadsworth Longfellow, from "Evangeline"

I know the exact moment my husband, Bob, and I decided to write about the Ocklawaha River. We were casting around for a new book idea after collaborating—me as the writer, Bob as the photographer—on books about education, southern history, ghost lore and true crime. We tried to think about things we knew, things we didn't know and things we wanted to know. So, it started with an interest in Florida's maritime heritage—in particular, steamboats. Before the explosion of shopping malls and housing developments, there were no real roads in Florida, just a few Native American trails. Florida is a peninsula, and people get around on the water. Florida's deepwater ports have always been marketplaces for a global economy. Within its borders, however, a warren of rivers provided access to the interior—hence, the steamboat era. We thought we would write about that.

On one steaming hot summer day in 2016, Bob and I took a trip to the Ocala National Forest to see one of the old steamboat landings, the Davenport. Particular sites in the Ocala National Forest are hard to pinpoint. We drove for over an hour, then a few miles down a dirt road before we turned onto a bumpy, two-rut track that ended on the banks of the lower Ocklawaha River.

At the trailhead, we saw a footpath, which we later found out led to a kiosk full of steamboat memorabilia. I presume people aren't supposed to live in the Ocala National Forest, but there were two hard-used tents pitched, supplies strewn about and a man fishing down by the river. We spoke to him briefly—and from upwind, because he smelled like a seasoned camper.

"A gator comes by every day around eleven o'clock," he said, pointing.

We scrambled down the bluff to get a better look. Sure enough, there was the gator, his hide a rough oval amid the shimmering waters of the river. Around him flowed the Ocklawaha.

For some reason, out of the maze of river networks in central and north Florida—Crystal, Withlacoochee, Indian, Matanzas, Rainbow, Weeki Wachee, Wakulla, Suwanee—the Ocklawaha took our fancy. It was dark and placid, its satiny surface dimpled by the light raindrops that had just begun to fall from the humid sky. Hyacinths floated like small green islands, and the river's banks were sandy. There was the shriek of red-shouldered hawks and the boisterous oinks of pig frogs. Most intriguing of all were the river's distinctive and elusive curves. There is nothing forthright about the Ocklawaha. Unlike the cascading mountain creeks to the north, it was quiet except for the distant sound of a motorboat and the burble of a deadhead log lifting and falling in the current. Its waters commence their own unique and twisted path, fading away into the mist like a memory.

Right then and there, without us knowing anything about its rich history, the river cast its spell on us. We were hooked. We wanted to know it, paddle it, motor on it, write about it. We weren't alone. People had always fished, hunted and explored the secret recesses of the river. Many people grew up canoeing, rafting and kayaking on it. Marjorie Kinnan Rawlings wrote about the river in her famous book *Cross Creek*. The Ocklawaha holds a place in the Floridian imagination as mystical as the river Styx, forging a boundary between earth and some other world.

PLANNING THE RIVER TRIP

We determined that we couldn't paddle the entire river, although we later met people who had done it. But the Upper Ocklawaha Basin contains all the waters that feed the Ocklawaha River upstream before the confluence with Silver River. The headwaters of the river are further into Central Florida, in Lake County, at the Harris chain of lakes (Apopka, Griffin, Dora, Eustis and Yale).

The green swamp area, an important headwater south of Apopka, is not easy to access by land, plus, Lake Apopka and Lake Griffin are among Florida's most polluted lakes. We didn't want to deal with blockages or traipsing across private poverty. Later, when we met Matt Keene, a documentary filmmaker and master kayaker, he said that the upper Ocklawaha is an enjoyable gentle paddle with a collection of water from some of the oldest sandhills in Florida. Still, we chose our starting point to be at the Silver Springs run, a nine-mile tributary, because although it was by no means entirely safe from algae blooms, it was, at least, consistently pristine.

From our proposed starting point, the river travels along the western and northern boundary of the Ocala National Forest before its union with the St. Johns River and, ultimately, the Atlantic Ocean at the seaport city of Jacksonville. We wanted to begin at the lower Ocklawaha basin, where the striped bass used to come in, and go to Putnam County, where the Ocklawaha empties into the St. Johns.

Like the St. Johns River, the Ocklawaha River is one of the few continental major rivers to flow northward. The river itself is mostly contained within Marion County, while its drainage basin strays into Alachua, Putnam and

Cypress knees.

Orange Counties. A sector of cypress swamp spreads from the water's edge to about fifteen feet above the water level. Then, there is a zone of hardwood hammock—mostly live oak, sabal palm and palmetto. Higher in elevation is the forest—mostly sand, pine and scrub oak.

In river miles, the distance from Silver Springs to the St. Johns River is approximately fifty-eight miles. It was an ambitious project for two amateurs with full-time jobs. Bob and I are not waterway or camping experts. We have spent the majority of our adult lives in North American suburbs. Suburbs are places where there may be an occasional foray into non-landscaped terrain, particularly after a hurricane, but in no way does this qualify as "roughing it." However, we were motivated, around this time, by our adult children, who decided to move in with us. It seemed opportune to indulge in the vital domestic concept of "space," especially as our interest in the Ocklawaha River required us to spend a lot of time exploring it.

HISTORY OF THE SEMINOLES ON THE OCKLAWAHA RIVER

We resolved to take our time and travel small segments of the serpentine watercourse with the name that translates to "crooked [or muddy, great or dark] waters"—a title given by the Native Americans who used the shady "creek" for transportation. At normal water level, particularly back then, the river would have been relatively clear, but deep shade was provided by the dense growth of canopied trees that leaned over the creek before it was timbered.

Its surrounding history entails—as most American history does—European men and their descendants appropriating the ancient hunting grounds of Native Americans going back to Da Gama and the Timucuans. Matters had not improved by the time a fateful meeting between Osceola, the Seminole chiefs and federal government agents occurred at Payne's Landing on the Ocklawaha in 1832. The government issued an ultimatum to the Indians, although they framed it as a "treaty." The treaty said the Seminoles had three years to move to Oklahoma, west of the Mississippi River.

Anyone familiar with the Trail of Tears knows it was common in those days for the federal government to forcefully relocate Native Americans multiple times as property was developed by white settlers across the United

States. The Seminole tribe objected to being moved away from land and waters they had inhabited from time immemorial. They viewed the use of the river as a source of their spiritual power. Osceola put a knife through the government treaty, and the second Seminole Indian War began in earnest. It lasted for years, with a devastating outcome for Native Americans, many of whom were imprisoned in the Castillo De San Marcos in St. Augustine, including Osceola (who later died of malaria while in captivity in the South Carolina prison at Fort Moultrie).

According to ghost tours in St. Augustine, Osceola's suffering visage is still visible on the exterior face of the southern side of the fortress wall. Tourists can see a more substantial likeness of Chief Osceola ripping through the white man's treaty in a statue that presides over a cove at Silver Springs State Park.

STEAMBOATS ON THE OCKLAWAHA

There were scores of steamboats on the St. Johns and the Ocklawaha Rivers in the late nineteenth and early twentieth centuries. Along the riverbanks are the remnants of many stops from the old steamboat line, which are now mostly boat launches.

Hubbard Hart, a white-mustachioed Yankee from Vermont who blockaded for the Confederacy in a steam-driven paddleboat, the *Silver Spring*, also cleared the Ocklawaha River for the Union after the Civil War. A commissioned officer in

Ocklawaha on the Ocklawaha River. *Florida Memories.*

the service of supply, moving cannons and military equipment, Hart called himself "Colonel" and lied to the government in a multipage letter, "To his Excellency Andrew Johnson, President of the United States," brazenly writing, "I have never been actively engaged in the Confederate service."

As a practical man (and one not overly concerned with scruples), some historians say Hart would have been another Henry Flagler if he'd had the financial backing. Hart started out buying a stagecoach line in Savannah, Georgia, in the 1850s. He bid on mail contracts in northeast Florida and

Colonel Hubbard Hart.
Museum of Florida History.

maintained a stage line between Tampa and Palatka. He often stopped at Silver Springs to water his horses. (He was one of many who came up with the idea of a rowboat "with a glass bottom.") From stagecoaches, he expanded to steamboats, and by 1883, Hart's "jungle tours," four-day roundtrip expeditions by steamboat from Palatka to Silver Springs, were advertised in *Harper's Magazine.*

Published articles in a national magazine brought more tourists. In those days, "social media" consisted of letters, and the people who toured the Ocklawaha River and Silver Springs wrote to their friends and family about the experience: the whirlpools, the abrupt turns, occasional forays against the trunks of trees. There were the sounds of animals and reptiles. It was the real Florida experience, the theme park for the nineteenth century, and it was delightfully warm in the winter. The word spread.

By 1885, Hart had added twelve boats to his fleet. To accommodate his burgeoning business, Hart devised a custom "shallow draft" paddleboat with the recessed wheel in the stern. It was low and long with a narrow-beamed hull that could navigate through the sometimes clogged and always winding river. One of his boats even introduced an "inclined engine" with compact, space-saving features. These boats were short, only between sixty and ninety feet in length. They never would have survived in the ocean, and they were much smaller than those that plied most North American rivers, even the St. Johns. The famous novelist Harriet Beecher Stowe refused to board one, saying it looked like "a gigantic coffin."

Steamboat enthusiasts did not share her views. Hart's unique rivercraft was featured at the 1892 Chicago World's Fair. A year or two later, a writer of the *Florida Annual* stated: "Leaving Florida without seeing the Ocklawaha is like leaving Rome without seeing the pope." In the closing decades of the nineteenth century, Hart's steamboats carried passengers and freight up and down the river to the area of the headwater lakes in north central Florida. It was a post office and a packet line that transported everything from oranges to silk hats; it was an excursion line for hunters who shot at game on the banks of the river by day.

Long before the Endangered Species Act, the Hart line provided the guns, and passengers blasted anything that moved—tropical birds, deer, gators. Porters went out in little boats to collect the game and gave it to the tourists

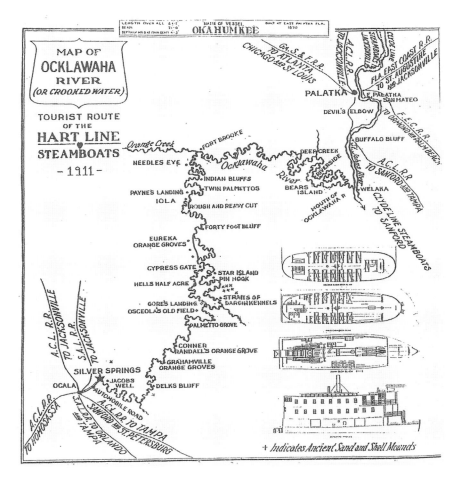

Tourist route of the Hart Line steamboats. *Florida Memories.*

to take home. By the 1880s, tropical birds were rare. Clifton Johnson, author of *Highways and Byways of Florida*, wrote in 1918: "One annoyance to sensitive persons on the old-time passenger boats was the constant firing of sportsmen's guns. These guns were in the hands of men who seemed to think that the chief end of man is to shoot something....Several shooting accidents to passengers, one of which resulted fatally, at last compelled a reform of the abuse."

The Hart line switched to wooden guns for the tourists who posed for pictures on the dock with giant stuffed gators. There was no shortage of passengers. Hundreds of tourists boarded steamboat excursions only to discover they were crammed into tight berthing quarters. Porters of small stature set up folding tables in the passageways so passengers could have a place to sit and eat. The fee for the trip was five dollars, which included a room and meals that usually featured wild turkey, venison, quail, chicken or farm-fresh eggs.

At night, passengers extolled the exotic experience as the wood-fueled vessels roiled along the dark waters lit only with pine-pitch torches. Bowmen with long poles would push back toward the middle of the river when the steamboat ran too close to the trees. Big metal cauldrons on top of the boat burned fat and wood day and night in an open fire, providing light. A passenger writing about it to a friend said in a letter:

> *The flickering yellow light gave an eerie appearance to the river and to the black swampy jungle; an eeriness enhanced by the mournful cries of hoot owls and the screams of bobcats. The light drew inquisitive wild creatures to the water's edge, and their eyes glowed in the darkness like red hot coals.*

Sidney Lanier, a poet, concurred with Stowe about the strange shape of the steamboat, calling it "a Pensacola gopher with a preposterously exaggerated back," and gave us a glimpse of what the Ocklawaha River was like 152 years ago, when he wrote about his trip on the *Marion*:

> *Presently we rounded the raft, abandoned the broad and garish highway of the St. Johns, and turned off to the right into the narrow lane of the Ocklawaha, the sweetest water-lane in the world, a lane which runs…betwixt hedgerows of oaks and cypress and palms and bays and magnolias and mosses and manifold vine growths, a lane clean to travel along for there is never a speck of dust in it save the blue and gold dust which the wind blows out of the flags and lilies, a lane which is as if a typical woods-stroll had taken shape and as if God had turned into water and trees the recollection of some meditative ramble through the lonely seclusions of His own soul.*

The *Marion*, where Lanier famously transcribed his poetic reflections, was originally owned by Captain Henry Gray. Hart dominated the Ocklawaha River with his popular excursions, but he was not free from competition. Gray, a former Confederate officer, sold the *Marion* to Hart in 1880 and worked for him as a pilot for over a decade.

Another competitor, Ed Lucas of Palatka, operated several vessels, providing Hart with some of his stiffest competition. After one of Lucas's boats sank, he suffered financial losses and flirted with bankruptcy, and in the end, he briefly merged his line with Hart's.

Another notable steamboat operator was James Hatton Howard, who came to Central Florida by way of North Carolina. Howard settled in Grahamville, a place, if it still existed today, that would be found on County Road 314, north of State Road 40, on the east side of the Ocklawaha River. It was known as a famous landing and has been the site of some fruitful archeological digs by scuba divers, yielding an intact bronze Spanish mission bell and a hand-hammered copper bowl.

William Howard on the Ocklawaha River. *Florida Memories*.

Howard had several steamboats on the river, with most of them named after members of his family, including the *Mary Howard* and *Sophia Howard*. The most famous of these, built in Palatka in 1903, was the *William Howard*. It was small—only eighty-five feet long—but was the only steamboat on the river with power steering. As a steamboat pilot, Howard was less interested in excursions than Hart was, although the *William Howard* was set up for at least fifteen guests at a time. The delivery of freight, mail and supplies, as well as local transportation up and down the river, generated the bulk of the company's profits. When James Hatton Howard died, his son James Hatton Howard II took on the family business.

The new steamboat pilot wrote an article for the *Motorboating Magazine* in 1942:

> *At the turn of the century my father operated a steamer on the Ocklawaha, but his death occurred shortly after I was graduated from Georgia Tech. As I always was fond of boats, I purchased the steamer [William Howard] from his estate and continued to keep her moving.*

James Hatton Howard II lived on the steamboat for two years until his sons became old enough for him to worry about them falling overboard. But it is clear that he loved the adventure of the river. Captain Howard II eventually wrote his memoirs, and this was where the story of a famous alligator named Oscar begins. The hapless reptile was caught up in the sternwheel paddle of the *William Howard*.

Oscar the alligator was renowned on the Ocklawaha River for showing up every afternoon to sun himself on a log and then dramatically diving under the *William Howard*. One day, Oscar didn't dive deep enough, and his enormous twelve-foot body became wedged into the engine machinery. According to Captain Howard, "There was a loud, jarring noise, and the engine groaned and ceased to turn." It took Howard and his crew five hours to pry the reptile loose, all the while keeping clear of the gator's powerful tail.

A river man appropriated Oscar, keeping him in a pen on the river. Eventually, there was a hurricane, and Oscar must have considered the weather a parole, because he swam free. The next day, he was back on his old log sunning himself. He still dived to entertain passengers, but he never got caught up in the stern paddlewheel again.

In 1907, the *William Howard* was sold and renamed the *Tourist*. The new owners went out of business within a year. James Hatton Howard II bought back the boat and, abandoning the passenger side of business, used it as a barge to help rebuild a railroad bridge over the St. Johns River in Jacksonville.

THE END OF THE STEAMBOAT ERA

Soon, the steamboat era was over—and not because the captains had hard competition when it came to the beauty of the route, which was unsurpassed. Their challenge was the utility of the route and the men of rails: David Yulee, Henry Plant and Henry Flagler. These men made impressive inroads in locomotive transportation; one charter on the South Florida Railroad train in Sanford, Florida, laid rail along a pier to pick up steamboat passengers at one of the landings on Lake Jessup. It seems, at least for a brief time, that this relationship might have been considered symbiotic. By the late nineteenth century, train lines in Palatka, Leesburg, Silver Springs and Fort Mason were hitting hard at the Hart and Howard routes.

But it wasn't the competition from trains that pushed Hart's and Howard's steamboats out of commission. It was the paved roads and highways and the golden age of the automobile. Hart died in 1895. His relatives eked out the steamboat business for another twenty-five years until it was no longer profitable.

Left: Derelict *Hiawatha* steamboat. *Right*: *Hiawatha* on the Ocklawaha River. *Florida Memories.*

James Hatton Howard II, of the *William Howard*, gave up the steamboat trade and moved to Daytona Beach in 1915. There, he opened a boatyard. His granddaughter Elizabeth Howard remembers going to his boatyard, Howard's Boatworks, to visit Zora Neale Hurston. The famous writer of *Their Eyes Were Watching God* used to dock there in her houseboat, the *Wanago*.

By the 1930s, all the steamboats, including the Hart and the Howard lines, were gone. The steamboats languished for decades, decaying hulks left stranded in canals or boatyards. They ended their days rotting in an abandoned dock or along the side of a bridge, raided for their wood, or until someone came along and set the wooden carcasses on fire.

In fact, for many years on the shore of Harts Point in East Palatka, the last and the largest of the inboard paddlewheel steamers on the Ocklawaha, the *Hiawatha*, was visible as drivers crossed the Veterans Memorial Bridge. In its heyday, the *Hiawatha*, the last of Hart's steamboats, was eighty-nine feet long and had about twenty-eight staterooms that each measured about thirty-five square feet and had two bunks. Ten of the cabins were on the middle deck, and eighteen were on the upper deck. The quarters could accommodate fifty-six passengers, twenty crew members (who slept in berths on the machinery deck) and about ten passengers who agreed to stand up or sleep on the deck. Although it was a two-day downstream trip, it took three days for the *Hiawatha* to push back against the upstream current from Palatka to Silver Springs.

But somewhere around the latter half of the 1910s, Hart's *Hiawatha* struck a submerged log, the hull split, and the boat sank to the bottom of the river. It is not known whether passengers were on board. Later, the boat was

Hiawatha steamboat mural in Palatka. *Sponsored by the Conlee Mural Committee; mural by Wendy Beeson.*

raised and towed to Palatka. I heard rumors that in the 1980s, more than sixty years after the boat sank, some teenagers threw their cigarettes on the steamboat's rotting deck and burned up the *Hiawatha*.

Donnie Adams, a lifelong Palatka resident, knows the real story. A big man, Donnie looks a little like the old pictures of Hubbard Hart. He owns a building where he and local people pursue their hobbies. In the nineteenth century, it was a big, old brick stable, and today, it accommodates Adams's boatbuilding projects and local artifacts. In it is all that remains of the *Hiawatha*—the legacy of Hart's steamboat era on the Ocklawaha.

The remains feature a lifeboat from the *Hiawatha* that is over one hundred years old. Adams says the dusty lifeboat is still in good enough shape to be restored and made water-worthy, and that's what he intends to do. That was not true for the grand steamboat from whence it came.

Standing outside his building and gesturing toward the bridge, Adams said, "The boat [*Hiawatha*] was rotten through and through; there was no restoring it. It had been in the water and it was full of water moccasins. George Smith, the man who bought the old Hart property, broke it down, piece by piece, and burned it."

One-hundred-year-old *Hiawatha* lifeboat. *Donnie Adams; photograph by Bob H. Lee.*

Hiawatha steamboat deck replica.
Florida Museum of History.

Although the steamboats are gone, the Florida Museum of History in Tallahassee built a full-size interactive reproduction of half the *Hiawatha* with a few of the original pieces taken from the beached remains before it was burned. The display recaptures some of the excitement and a lot of the history of the bygone steamboat industry on the Ocklawaha River.

THE CROSS-FLORIDA BARGE CANAL

The potential exploitation of the river's natural beauty wasn't confined to a steamboat line or two. Federal and local governments campaigned to raise funds to effectively cut Florida in half to create the Cross-Florida Barge Canal. Merchants and the military thought this was a good idea that would allow them to avoid the long trip around the peninsula. Proponents saw it as a passageway for national defense and a pathway that would secure job growth and economic development. As a result, the U.S. Army Corps of Engineers targeted thousands of acres of uplands and riverine swamps, the accompanying wildlife and the Ocklawaha River itself for decimation. The planned course of the canal trailed the St. Johns River from the Atlantic shoreline to Palatka to the basin of the Ocklawaha River, and then the Withlacoochee River to the Gulf of Mexico.

Federal campaigns to dig up harbors and rivers were far from rare. According to Rachel Carson in her book *Silent Spring*, a project seriously considered by engineers of the Panama Canal involved "low yield nuclear explosions…for the instant construction of a sea-level channel…with a string of precisely timed detonations."

By comparison, Florida's project and this experiment with its landscape and topography was nothing new; it was an idea toyed with as far back as 1567 by Philip II of Spain. It was also the subject of numerous governmental studies, many of them funded by President Franklin D. Roosevelt in the 1930s. Canal funding proceeded sporadically throughout the Roosevelt administration and aimed to provide work for the Civilian Conservation Corps. However, in 1938, the canal project was shut down by a Republican senator from the Midwest who described it as a waste of taxpayer money.

Cross-Florida Barge Canal, west coast.

The zombie-like canal project kept adapting and reviving. Work on the canal was reauthorized in 1942. Lyndon Baines Johnson, known for his "Great Society" social-services programs, finally initiated the barge canal kickoff in the 1960s.

Mike Stallings, a well-known archeologist who grew up in Palatka, says he remembers the day Johnson came to Palatka. As a president who favored large public-works endeavors, Johnson allocated $1 million to restart the barge canal project and said, in 1964, "God…gave us great natural estuaries, natural locales for harbors, but he left it to us to dredge them out for use by modern ships."

Stallings, a tall, soft-spoken man, described that day and said that all the schools closed to commemorate the event:

> *It was a rainy day. We were told there was big money coming in with these barges, there'd be jobs for everyone. So, the parents and all the kids showed up and they had this big stage with other dignitaries standing up on it. Johnson was giving a little talk, but I couldn't get a good view of him. Me and a friend climbed up a tree, but the Secret Service came and made us get down. Then Johnson mashed a button, and—understand that bags of flour were on top of the dynamite, so it would be more scenic—and the dynamite blew up and then the president got on his helicopter and flew off.*

The route of the projected canal was a whopping 107 miles from Palatka on the St. Johns River to Yankeetown on the west coast of Florida (the Panama Canal is only 48 miles). The strategy was to dam the river at two points, raising the water level to accommodate immense barges, which would cross-commute through Florida to get from the Gulf of Mexico to the Atlantic Ocean. Then, the Army Corps of Engineers would go on to "flood 27,350 acres of hardwood forest to create a shallow barge canal and a reservoir that would provide its regular water supply."

The wastage of timber was next. Brown Gregg, a Leesburg engineer, created the infamous "tree crusher"—an iron beast that weighed twenty-two tons, floated in eight feet of water and could take down half a dozen or more old-growth cypress trees at a time. Workers offered the final *coup de grace* by drenching the massive debris piles in diesel fuel and igniting them. According to "The Final Impact Statement For the Ocklawaha River Restoration Project, Marion and Putnam Counties," by the United States Department of Agriculture, "approximately 2,040 acres were cleared" with this odious contraption.

The passage to nowhere—the bridge canal cut for the unfinished Cross-Florida Barge Canal project intended to connect the Gulf of Mexico and the Atlantic Ocean across Florida for barge traffic. Two sections were built, but the project was cancelled, mainly for environmental reasons and its status as a $100 million boondoggle.

Mike Stallings witnessed the tree crusher. He said:

> *It was a massive machine. They called it "the monster." It was a huge piece of equipment on two tracks, with a wheelhouse on the top of it, and they used that to drive out through the woods and crush the trees down. And that's what they did around the area the canal was built. They leveled the land. Back then, the river was still within its banks because the dam hadn't been built yet. They gutted the forest. Tree stumps sticking up everywhere. Then they find out the canal wasn't wide enough to float two barges side by side. And it wasn't deep enough for your big barges.*

In the end, the Army Corps of Engineers built about one-third of the 107-mile project. The Cross-Florida Barge Canal led to the annihilation of nine thousand acres of sensitive habitat along sixteen miles of the Ocklawaha. There was also the waste of millions of taxpayer dollars and, finally, the bitterly contested Rodman dam (officially named "Kirkpatrick Dam" to honor Florida state senator George Kirkpatrick, who fought for years to keep it) that blocked the Ocklawaha River ten miles upstream from its

The front of Rodman dam.

The back of Rodman dam.

confluence with the St. Johns River. In 1968, the earthen dam was built across the Ocklawaha River with four spillway gates, creating the Rodman reservoir. The dam brought on the rise of ecological activism in Florida, led by a self-effacing Micanopy zoologist named Marjorie Harris Carr.

MARJORIE HARRIS CARR AND THE BIRTH OF THE FLORIDA DEFENDERS OF THE ENVIRONMENT

Marjorie Harris Carr was a local girl who graduated from Fort Myers High School in 1932 and went to Florida State University when it was still called the Florida State College for Women. She graduated with a bachelor of science degree in zoology and became the first federal female wildlife technician in Florida.

According to her biographer, Peggy Macdonald, the job "introduced her to two future loves": the Ocklawaha River, where she collected samples, and her future husband, Archie Carr, a herpetologist famous for his work documenting the migration patterns of sea turtles. Marjorie and Archie lived apart for the first year of marriage so that she could keep her job. By necessity, her marriage was a secret. Married female technicians were unheard of in the late 1930s.

Eventually, with Archie's help, Marjorie was able to attend the graduate program at the University of Florida, which was still primarily an all-male institution, and in 1942, she received her master of science in zoology. Ironically, that was the same year Congress authorized construction of the Cross-Florida Barge Canal and the destruction of the Ocklawaha River.

By 1971, after $74 million in taxpayer dollars had already been spent on the construction of the proposed Cross-Florida Barge Canal, Marjorie Harris Carr, founder of the Florida Defenders of the Environment (FDE), put a halt to the government's destruction. She and a troop of environmental activists stopped the Army Corps of Engineers from cutting Florida in half and destroying the Ocklawaha River.

Because of Carr's and FDE's activism, President Richard Nixon halted the construction of the canal, calling the Ocklawaha River "a national treasure." Nixon was not exactly the heroic spokesman the FDE envisioned, but he was instrumental in ultimately saving the Ocklawaha River. However, the Rodman dam still stands. It is, among other things, a symbol of a protracted environmental conflict in Florida's history.

The dam is the bane of existence for the FDE. The controversy over the Rodman dam still rages to this day, so much so that opponents have considered blowing it up, as noted in Macdonald's book, *Marjorie Harris Carr: Defender of Florida's Environment*:

> *Late in his life, David Anthony, a University of Florida professor...gave serious thought to blowing up Rodman dam....David reasoned that by the time the authorities got around to prosecuting him, he would be dead.*

Other environmental activists also entertained notions of a huge blast that would end the imposition of the dam across the Ocklawaha River. It was their leader, Marjorie Harris Carr, who insisted, "That's not the way to do it."

THE FUTURE OF THE OCKLAWAHA RIVER

The portion of the river originally designated for the barge canal is now named after Marjorie Harris Carr. Created out of the debacle that was to be the Cross-Florida Barge Canal, today, the Marjorie Harris Carr Cross Florida Greenway is state-controlled land and the corridor for recreational kayaking and boating on the Ocklawaha River. Carr created a chapter in Florida's environmental history that ensured the river is still here and relatively intact.

Still, a serious impediment for a free-flowing river (and an unimpeded route down the Ocklawaha) is the Rodman dam, which blocks boat travel and the river's free flow. Donnie Adams, owner of the one-hundred-year-old lifeboat from the steamship *Hiawatha*, remembers the last time he and his father and brother drove their ski boat from Silver Springs to Palatka:

> *My father tells my brother, "I'm going to let Donnie drive the boat all the way back down the river." I thought, "Wow!" It was like handing me the keys to a spaceship or something. So, I drove all the way back, and we got back in the evening right at sundown to the mouth of the river. My father sits there, and he said to me and my brother, "I want you to remember this. Remember it, because nobody else will have this. They're closing the river at six o'clock in the morning. You'll never get to drive the Ocklawaha again without that barrier being there." They had built the dam, and the next day, they closed the river off. I never thought to thank my Dad until after he died. He gave me the present of driving the Ocklawaha one last time.*

A practical and a political way to breach the Rodman dam has not yet emerged, although it is a frequent and rancorous topic of discussion in Marion County and the subject of an ingenious lawsuit filed by the Florida Defenders of the Environment (FDE) in 2017 against the U.S. Forestry Service in Putnam County regarding lapsed permits.

Recently, a new plan has emerged from the John H. Hankinson Ocklawaha Legacy Fund. Hankinson died in March 2017, and according to the FDE website, his "professional career revolved around the inter-relationship of land and water resources, protecting watersheds to assure there would be clean and abundant water in the future."

The new plan created in his name is called the "Silver Ocklawaha Blueway Action Plan." It proposes reestablishing Hart's historic steamboat route from Silver Springs to Palatka by creating a connection at the

Great blue heron on Silver River.

Rodman dam to allow the passage of people, fish and manatees. The plan does not destroy the dam or disrupt the annual bass fishing tournament at the Rodman Reservoir. It also does not allow the Ocklawaha River to flow freely; it is just a minor gateway. However, it is a start, and if implemented, it would provide a small compromise and perhaps a crack in the opposition from the "Save Rodman Dam" proponents, whose idea of conservation, as E.O Wilson would have it, "is stocking trout streams and planting trees around golf courses."

Yet, it is important to note that there are serious and credible advocates for keeping the Rodman dam in place. The passion for the reservoir is just as elevated as that of the advocates who favor breaching the dam. It's a matter of self-identification. If you consider yourself a fisherman and earn your income by taking people fishing on Rodman Reservoir, you are almost certainly going to be pro-dam.

Despite so much controversy, the river endures, ageless in its mystery and its beauty. Bob and I were keenly aware that in the two years it would take us to write the book and photograph the river, we could never approach the level of knowledge held by people who have lived on or around the Ocklawaha River and fought for its survival. I call our book a literary documentary because, in the end, any river is a narrative in which the voices of those who love it dissolve into one sound: the language of free-flowing water.

Our goal is that this book incorporates the sound of seasoned voices as well as our own novice ones. In fact, we hope the book is a giant shout-out that will attract the attention the river deserves.

It is of vital significance to the survival of the river—and the survival of the accompanying wildlife and foliage—to incorporate a new generation of leaders who are receptive to the interests of the public and are willing to take control of the discussion about an ecological future for the Ocklawaha River.

The story of the Ocklawaha River is ultimately an endemic portrayal of Florida's natural history.

Part I

DAY TRIPS

1

SILVER RIVER

December 31, 2016

Going up that river was like traveling back to the earliest beginnings of the world, when vegetation rioted on the earth and the big trees were kings.
—*Joseph Conrad,* Heart of Darkness

A river is a simile. It flows like time; it fluctuates like history. The Ocklawaha has existed as a river for thousands of years. It may be the oldest flowing river in Florida.

At one time, rivers functioned as highways and interstates. Florida had more land mass in earlier days, and over time, the course of the river ping-ponged a bit, broadened or narrowed by drought, obstructions and hurricanes. There are archeological sites throughout that contain dugout canoes, boilers from steamboats and even mastodon and saber-tooth cat bones. Native people once paddled dugout canoes, marked trees to determine who or what lurked in its tributaries and made tools and weapons from flint, stone and wood. The river provided the native people with water and food. They cooked and heated fish and game with burning shells.

The river is the site of warlike events, too. As mentioned in the introduction, the treaty of Payne's Landing was negotiated on the Ocklawaha, and it was there that Chief Osceola, a Seminole Indian, took his final stand. He thought of his tribe as *yat'siminoli*, or free people, and he died trying to preserve their freedom.

There is a famous 1930s crime site on the river. A country road north of the Ocklawaha River once led to the bullet-ridden house of Ma Barker and her gangster son Fred. The pair died at dawn in a shootout with FBI men during a blazing gun battle. The infamous pair were found dead with their machine guns by their sides.

These events added context and made my husband, Bob, and me eager to unfurl the mystery of the Ocklawaha River. However, our desire did not entail blind love. Paddling in the spring or the summer with the heat and the mosquitos and the mating alligators was not appealing. So, we waited until New Year's Eve Day. During an unusually warm Florida winter, we unwittingly picked the coldest day of the year.

Bob and I, along with our friend Jack Bass, planned to canoe upstream on the Silver River to Silver Springs and back downstream to the mouth of the Ocklawaha, a ten-mile paddle round-trip. Jack and his wife, Darlene (who had sensibly stayed home), have been our camping buddies for the past twenty years. We met when our children were in preschool, and two more unlikely couples could not have become close companions. Politically, we were at odds on every issue, and we politely deferred such discussions. Jack and Darlene were native Floridians, and Jack was a seasoned outdoorsman with an avid interest in Florida history. He, unlike us, knew how to handle himself equally well on terrain and in the water. In his trademark Orlando Magic baseball cap, he was a compact man with a barrel chest and the strength of an ox. I had seen him head a group of kayakers for many miles on Crystal River, pushing through the water with strong strokes while other paddlers tired and fell back.

On New Year's Eve in 2016, we left from Ray Wayside Park in eastern Marion County just off State Road 40. It was 7:30 a.m. and thirty-two

Jack's canoe at Ray Wayside Landing.

Silver River from Ray Wayside Landing.

degrees. I was warm enough in thermals, boots, a cap, a sweatshirt and a coat. But my gloves were useless—my fingers frozen, aching with arthritis.

A layer of fog hung above the Silver River. The reflection of cypress trees wavered in the water. Jack climbed into the back of the canoe; I manned the middle. Bob pushed us off and jumped into the bow to complete our threesome. We paddled upstream through a haze unfurling in ghostly plumes, the water blue beneath the white canoe, the sky a flat gray wash punctuated by sunbeams that made the water vapor prism and dance. The tip of the canoe seemed to part the mist billowing on either side. We could not see more than a few inches ahead. It was quiet without so much as a birdcall. The only sound was our oars dipping and rising into the river water, propelling us toward a horizon we could not see.

What we could see, below the mist, was a mirror of trees. Cypress knees ringed with previous water levels lined the banks of the river. Sunbeams began to peep through leafy gaps, touching the river with translucent fingers. The silhouette of a bird, wings upturned, fluttered among the shadows. We plunged on into the drifting mist.

A rooster crowed from far away. Birds began to appear on the river, roosting in trees, perched on fallen or broken limbs, wings outstretched and drying or sometimes rising, diving and skating across the water with exuberant energy. A grayish-blue flash caught my eye, and at first, I did not realize what it was until I saw it perch on the brittle limb of a wax myrtle. A moment later, the kingfisher skittered across the surface and deftly picked up a tiny minnow. None of these creatures were skittish at the sight of us, even though we clearly were in their domain. I figured they'd become acclimated to the sight of people talking, splashing and laughing.

Their domain was a world apart from the manicured lawns, golf courses and retention ponds of suburban Florida. Jack pointed out birds I'd never seen before: limpkin, anhinga and a pair of colorful wood ducks. My favorite was the cormorant, with its slightly hooked beak and vulture eyes that followed us without fear. There were herons and the egrets, as well, and tiny sparrows that hopped from branch to branch. The mud turtles began to appear, stretching out their yellow-striped heads toward the sun, a distant orb that glowed diffusely through the mist-shrouded sky. We saw a turtle the size of a fifty-cent piece sunning on a branch half submerged in the water.

We passed hatched aerial apple snail eggs on reeds above the water. The female snail leaves the water to lay her eggs on a stem of a plant, a trunk, a rock or any other hard object. It is a miracle the delicate apple snail can survive the tumult of the river or the appetites of the limpkins who feed on them.

As we paddled, Jack talked about growing up on the river fifty-five years ago:

> *The river is part of my childhood. I grew up in the woods and on the water. Some of my earliest memories are of the Ocala National forest and the Ocklawaha. My grandfather was very big into hunting and fishing. So, every weekend we would leave Melrose in whatever dilapidated automobile we had and make our way to Orange Springs. We'd go across on the ferry and go into where our camp was. The ferry's not there anymore, but you can put a boat in there; it's a launch.*

We stopped for a minute to rest. At first there was silence, then a faint echoing conversation among the birds. Bob stood up, rocking the canoe. "Mind if I cast a line?"

Jack said, "Go ahead."

Bob spun his reel and flung the line in the water.

Anhinga at sunrise.

Jack said, "The river, of course, is a lot wider now than it was then—back then, you could almost throw a rock across it."

Bob fished—fruitlessly, it seemed. Jack watched and ruminated:

Back then, the boats they had aren't like the boats they have now. You didn't get in a boat and go one hundred miles in a day. We were fishing in a flat-bottomed johnboat my grandfather made. It had a small kicker on it, probably less than twenty horsepower. We put the boat in at Moody's Landing, which was the closest landing to where his camp was, a little north of Pinner Pond, which is still there.

Bob asked, "Any crabs in these waters?"

Jack laughed. "Grandpa ran the crab traps he made. We'd get lots of crabs, big blue crabs. Crabs can no longer get up in this part of the river because of the Rodman dam."

Bob smoothly recast his line. "What about fish?"

Jack nodded vigorously and said:

Oh, we fished. Grandpa knew where the logjams were. Back years and years ago, probably the 1800s, they logged that whole area. They went in and cut all the big cypress trees down and floated them out of the Ocklawaha into the St. Johns, and from there, probably to Palatka to a sawmill. A lot of the logs didn't make it out. They either sank, or they got tangled up. Loggers made a train of these logs and tied them together, lashed them together, and snaked them outta the river.

This information jived with my own research, including a harrowing chapter in Marjorie Kinnan Rawlings's book, *South Moon Under*, in which the protagonist herded a train of logs downstream during a hurricane. There was more current local precedence, as well. A Marion County resident, Greg Chapman, joined the reality-based series *Ax Men*, which filmed logging operations across the country and featured the lower Ocklawaha in its seventh season. Turn-of-the-twentieth-century wood is worth several thousand dollars, and in one episode, they retrieved a "double-barrel," a Y-shaped log.

In the past and the present, people have gotten those logs up off the bottom of the river and sold them because they're pecky cypress. Locals call them deadheads. In 2013, there was a huge illegal deadhead logging case made on Rodman Lake. The case involved $350,000 of illegal timber seized by game wardens, which resulted in four felony counts against the tree poachers. Taking these logs illegally is stealing from the state.

"State charges a fee to deadhead log in certain places," Jack said. "Grandpa and I, we'd get anchored upstream from where the logjams were—they were like pick-up sticks on the bottom of the river. Vegetation would grow on them. It was like a freshwater reef. Red-eared sunfish, blue gills, speckled perch, catfish, occasional bass."

Anhinga at Silver River.

Bob snorted and sat back down in the canoe. "Not working today."

We all took up our paddles and dug into the flat water. Jack continued, "We would take those fish and clean 'em back at the camp. Grandpa would take a bottle cap, nail it to the end of a stick and scale fish with it. Over the years, the fish scales built up to where his fish-cleaning area, you didn't stand on dirt, you stood on fish scales that got higher and higher like a mini Indian burial mound."

I asked, "Did you have a refrigerator at your Grandpa's camp?"

Jack said:

> *We had freezers. My grandmother would take half-gallon milk jugs and open the top of them up, and wash 'em out and we would take the cleaned fish, put 'em in the milk jug, all the way up to where you could close it. She'd fill it up with water, reseal it and freeze it. So we had fresh frozen fish all year long. Back then, if you lived here in Florida, you lived off the land. You didn't go to the grocery store. Every meal we had was something that was caught, something that was hunted, something that was grown, something that was gathered.*

While listening to Jack, we hadn't noticed that the sun was almost up. People began to pass us in paddleboats, canoes and kayaks. We passed a gator headed for the old jungle exhibit, which we briefly toured from the water. Fake storefronts and crumbling forts. People used to see Silver Springs as a moneymaker instead of a natural resource.

Jack said:

> Before the Ocklawaha was dammed, those fish, they can smell water. They taste the water, they know where they're going. And they would go up into Silver Springs. Now, the water is more tannic, and it kills that. Plus, a lot of the springs don't flow anymore. If they ever got rid of the [Rodman] dam, and the water was allowed to flow freely, you'd get a lot more fish up in here. The shad have a run, but they can only go so far.

By this time, we were in Silver Springs, the sun was out, and the water reflected its sharp little shards, which glittered like a broken mirror. I had given Bob an underwater camera for Christmas, and he filmed the three statues sixty feet below, banked on the bottom of an underwater cliff.

"The statues," Bob said, "were props for that old television show *Sea Hunt?* With Lloyd Bridges."

Later, when I looked it up, I saw that Bob was partially right; *Sea Hunt* was filmed at Silver Springs—for years, the park hosted an annual underwater knife fight, with the aquatic actors each trying their best to sever the other's air hose.

But the statues were, in fact, leftover from the 1960s show *I Spy*, which starred Bill Cosby and Richard Culp. The sunken, bearded "spy" statues were covered with algae as late as 2014, but now they were clean and easily recognizable in the clear blue-and-pink-dappled water. I don't know why there is always pink streaking the blue underwater color of the springs, but I hope it is not because of pollution, because the rosy dots and beams are quite beautiful.

We passed a glass-bottom tourist boat and waved. The captain gestured down the river. "There's manatees ahead." We quickly paddled onward. Sighting a manatee in its natural environment is, for us, as exciting as a safari for large-animal enthusiasts. We had done it enough to spot the telltale signs—a plethora of eel grass and the brief sight of the sea cow's limpid eyes and large nostrils. Manatees come up for air a few times an hour. Bob and I have seen them at Blue Springs in Volusia County and in Crystal River in Citrus County, hundreds and hundreds of them lying side by side at the bottom of the river. These old sea beasts, which look as though they're descended from elephants, spend a lot of time sleeping. But it was early morning, the air was chill and the Silver River was not rife with the gray mammals because of the locks and dams. But we got lucky.

Bob pointed ahead. "There they are," he said.

From a distance, they looked like two lazy mermaids. The sunlight created a patterned grid on their immense bodies, and they glided through the water with their absurd tiny flippers and then floated like fat clouds in synch through the blue water. There was a rhythm to their movement, something innate, watery and prehistoric. It seemed like a miracle that such immense animals could possess such grace. They churned the bottom silt with their immense paddle-shaped tails, snuffled along the sand, chewed eel grass, floated with their mouths full to the surface to inhale air and then plunged back into their liquid turquoise world beneath the hull of our canoe. There were big fat bubbles like the ones that floated in *Sea Hunt*. The manatees drifted, accompanied by silvery fish and turtles whose innate submerged grace was also belied by their clumsy endeavors above the water.

We passed an abandoned wooden houseboat, its paint flaked and peeling. There was more traffic on the river, and at one point, a couple in a canoe ran right into us. There was a tense moment. In a British accent, the man stiffly said, "European traffic rules on the river."

Then, he pushed off without another word. I felt like saying, "You're on my side of the pond now, mate." But I didn't. That's not in my nature.

Most people on the river just wave and say hello or ask for directions.

By the time the Brits had passed, Bob had called out, "There's manatees ahead," and everyone was energized.

"Where?"

"On the left side of the bank."

"Thanks."

We spotted an otter behind a tree and watched it lope, ferret-like, back to the water, where it dived beneath the cypress roots.

Silver River is clear as glass, and someone once described it to me as "the most beautiful sight I've ever seen." Certainly, the ability to *see* underwater creatures in their natural habitat is a unique and transforming experience. Sunlight has a different quality in clear waters, persuading the underworld to give up its secrets and shadows.

We paddled past Ray Wayside Park to look at the juncture where the Ocklawaha confluences with Silver River. The waters were dark, the way

Statues on the bottom of Silver Springs. Daily Telegraph.

twisted with bends and curves. A century and a half ago, Sidney Lanier, aboard the steamboat *Marion*, looked down into the river in the exact same spot and wrote:

> *The water of the Ocklawaha, which had before seemed clear enough, had now transitioned to a muddy stream as it flowed side by side, unmixing for some distance, with the Silver Spring water.*

The river was really crowded by now, with kayaks, canoes and paddleboats all headed for Silver Springs, the popular tourist spot.

"You done good," Jack Bass said, and Bob and I modestly smiled as we beached the canoe and lifted our gear out of the hull. Our next trip would be up the Ocklawaha in kayaks to Eureka Landing and its aborted dam. We hoped to go during the first weekend in March 2017.

We felt confident we could tackle the river on our own next time.

Maybe we were too confident.

2

THE FIRST FIVE MILES
OF THE OCKLAWAHA RIVER

February 5, 2017

"La Belle Riviere," he breathed, his voice almost an amorous croon.
—*James Alexander Thom,* Follow the River

It was a Saturday, and we needed to do housework and grocery shopping, bill-paying and numerous other tedious tasks that middle-class, middle-aged working people need to do on the weekend. When I mentioned to Bob that maybe we should spruce up the yard, he grimaced and turned to me with a signature look.

Bob said, "Let's go to the river tomorrow."

"Okay," I said. Immediately, I felt my mood brighten.

What was it about the Ocklawaha River that compelled us, drew us to it the way no other river had? All we knew was that slipping into those waters and riding the artery of the current soothed something inside of us—more than soothed; it fed something, made us a temporary part of something greater, wilder and more important than our day-to-day activities of earning a living and maintaining a home. The river restored something in us and awakened fragments of dreams half-remembered, as though we walked through life in a somnambulant state, and only on these waters were we awake and alive.

Our only responsibility was to reach a destination, and it would take muscle, patience and stamina to do it.

We thought this would be an easy trip. We knew where to put in the kayaks—at Ray Wayside Park in Marion County. Only, this time, at the end of the slip with the high root-veined banks and the green borders of spatterdock water lilies with tight yellow buds, we would turn left instead of right. We'd go under the Delks Bluff bridge and paddle at least five miles downstream from the mouth of the Silver River.

At 9:30 a.m., there was still a light fog floating an inch above the water of the river. We put the kayaks in amid a few other canoes and a pontoon boat, all going to Silver River. When we turned left and paddled through water vapor toward the Ocklawaha River, we were completely alone. A clinging dampness freshened our skin, and it felt good and clean. I paused for a moment to dip my hand into the warm, spring-fed water.

If Silver River is blue and pink, I would have to say the Ocklawaha is primarily green and gold. The water was surprisingly clear, and we could often see right down to the bottom, where dark fish—bream, probably—indolently swam. Right from the start, the abundance of wildlife was noticeably less on the Ocklawaha than it was on Silver River. The weather may have been partially responsible. It was in the fifties, with a dull gray blanket of clouds covering the sky. Trees dripped. Water bugs skated over the smooth waters. Seeds that looked like the wisps of a dandelion skeleton brushed past our faces.

We saw a great blue heron patiently stalking the shallows for fingerling fishes. A couple of limpkins and cormorants perched on the sturdy branches of a nearby tree and studied us. There were two wood ducks, a pair; I knew by now that wood ducks mate for life. We saw no manatees. There didn't seem to be as much eel grass as we saw in the Silver River. We wondered if the lack of wildlife was a result of the Rodman dam and all the locks. According to the "Save Rodman Dam" organization, a lot of the wildlife has congregated around the dam itself.

This is not to say that the Ocklawaha River is not beautiful and, above all, compelling. We literally slid like a spool of silk, carried by the river under the Delks Bluff bridge, where traffic from State Road 40 rumbled above us. We passed a man who lived under the bridge. He had a small trash fire burning, and he was putting a fishing line in the water. A half-mile down, three men were clustered around a picnic table littered with beer bottles. A cooler yawned open, and a brown canoe bobbed from the end of a rope. They shouted at me, "C'mon, girl, pick up the pace."

Seriously? I objected to the "girl" jibe; I was sixty-two years old, after all. But I am no slouch, and "pace" was the wrong word to say to a woman who has run 10K races in under an hour. I tightened my grip on my paddle, set my jaw and thought, "I'm just gettin' started."

Reflection of trees in the Silver River.

A half mile farther, we saw a small inshore boat, the *Ocklawaha Queen*, motor by. The pilot was behind a plastic tarp, wearing a hoodie, and had his face hidden. I wondered if he was a poacher.

There was some wake, and we bobbed like buoys. I wondered if our flimsy kayaks would swamp. In the old steamboat days, when two ships had to pass each other, one ducked into a channel. According to placards posted

Great blue heron on the Ocklawaha River.

on trees up and down both sides of the river and proclaiming "BOUNDRIES," motorboats, fishing and alcohol were prohibited. All told, we saw about four boats—two of them dinghies, all with motors and fishing lines—on the Marjorie Harris Carr Cross Florida Greenway. Bob and I were on the exact stretch of river that Carr and the FDE had saved from decimation.

Our kayaks are yellow plastic, Potomac Pathfinders, ten feet long, the cheapest in the line, but they have the advantage of being extremely light, easy to carry and serviceable. We typically carry them on a tie-down rack atop Bob's 2000 Nissan Maxima. Because they're so light and rudderless, they are capable of flying over the surface of the water. They also have a tendency to spin and fecklessly go where the river wants them to go, not where *we* want to go. This could make still and video footage difficult to capture and dizzying.

As the miles melted away, Bob reminded me that paddling upstream was going to be considerably more challenging no matter how light our kayaks were. "We better rest up a bit first," he said. We began looking for a place to stop for lunch. We wanted to find a landmark, a place we could spot on a map and come back to on our next trip downstream.

We planned to keep marking these distances and keep going until, eventually, we would reach Putnam County.

At around 11:30 a.m., we found a small sliver of beach probably five or six miles down the river. The sand was near white and stuck to our sneakers. We climbed up the embankment to an area with a wooden bench, orange trees and an expanse of greenery. We walked down a path rimmed by barbed wire and an old house, which looked deserted. We peered out at the road, at the street signs—49th and 112th Streets. Two young boys zipped by us on dirt bikes. There was no one else around. It was probably private property and wouldn't do for a drop-off point. We would have to find a nearby boat launch for next time.

We picked an orange, shared it and ate our chicken salad sandwiches and chips sitting on the bench overlooking the river. We were alone, as we were during most of the trip. No boats went by, but we heard a multitude of birds—it was as though we were in the middle of Tarzan's jungle. The sky was still gray, the air moist. The green river lay before us, with the hyacinths framing it and our yellow kayaks awaiting our return. Sidney Lanier, the poet, wrote in 1875, aboard the *Marion* steamboat: "The lucent current lost all semblance of water. It was simply a distillation of many-shaded foliage's smoothly sweeping along beneath us. It was green trees, fluent." I felt a fragile connection to the past, knowing he had traveled these same waters over one hundred years ago.

We put in at around noon for the return trip, and the river didn't exactly fight us, but the current, which was moving at around one to two miles an hour and had so effortlessly carried us to our idyllic picnic, was now against us. If we didn't paddle, we went backward or spun around in our feather-light kayaks. We managed to shrug off our jackets, because we were now sweating in the cool center of the river. The smell of the river—earth, moisture, growing things and decaying things—was strong.

The Ocklawaha River twists and turns so much that at each bend, the current shoved us toward the water lilies and what there was of a bank, requiring a flurry of effort just to stay on our route. Bob found there were spots in the river where the current wasn't as intense, and we followed those slim, watery lines. But when the river narrowed, the current intensified, and it was a battle to gain distance. Algae-covered tree limbs loomed like gators. In some places, the river path was partially blocked by logjams, and the current swirled around the dense objects. At one point, Bob got stuck on a tree branch and had to push off, hard, to free the kayak.

We saw firsthand that the bottom of the Ocklawaha was littered with deadheads. We passed trees that had been struck by lightning; these had roots that, over the years, had become unearthed and climbed and bent and shaped themselves around the shattered trunk like huge wooden serpents. In fact, the erosion of the river had cut the roots and trees into strange twisted contours up and down the banks. There was also dried vegetation in the shapes of birds, as though the ghosts of generations past persisted amidst the vibrant growth and relentless current of the live river.

The sun finally came out, and Bob said he began to hear the traffic from the bridge. "It's just a few more bends," he said. This time, we waved to the people fishing off the banks and asked them how they did. They shrugged. Bob said he'd seen some bass striking schooling bait fish. The partying men were still ringed around their picnic table, and there was the smell of a campfire. They cheered when they saw us, and we managed to wave, but our arms ached from fighting the current.

When we reached the confluence of the Silver and the Ocklawaha Rivers, we found a couple in a johnboat with a failing motor and one paddle fighting the current to get back to Ray Wayside Park. I wished there was something we could have done to help other than shout spirited encouragement. But, given the diminutive size of our craft and an obvious lack of towing power, we left them with a friendly wave and pulled ahead. Bob skirted around the upstream side of the Ocklawaha, which was just as still and stagnant as a pond. Perhaps when it rains, there's more of a current.

So, after three and a half hours of paddling upstream, we finally pulled in to Ray. A family was fishing in the spot where the canoes and kayaks launch, but they moved over so we could get out and pull our kayaks up the ramp, use the restroom and pile the kayaks on the roof of Bob's old Nissan.

It was 3:30 p.m. A little while later, we saw a pontoon boat towing the stranded couple in the johnboat.

Even though it was cloudy, and Bob and I wore hats, the next day, our faces were sunburned. We had cantered the pulse of a natural conduit as casually as taking a live wire in our hands.

We would have to think of a better way to ride this river.

3

GORES LANDING TO EUREKA

March 5, 2017

Rivers derive their character from the environment.
—Charles R. Boning

B ob and I had been plotting the parameters of our next trip. Or rather, Bob had, and I gave him encouragement. To really cover some ground, he determined that the next leg of our trip down the Ocklawaha had to be twenty-six miles long. We would take two cars and park one at a northern landing in Eureka. Then, we could drive the other car back to put in at Ray Wayside Park again, but this time, we would pass the spot where we stopped for lunch and just keep going.

This plan had its pros and cons. On the pro side, it was immeasurably better than our brainstorm, which was to park on the side of a street, drag our kayaks over barbed wire and then traipse a half-mile over what may very well be private property down to the beachhead where we ate lunch. Another pro was that by using two cars, we wouldn't have to paddle upstream for hours to get back to one car.

On the con side was kayak portage, as only one car was outfitted with tie-down racks. Also, we had never paddled twenty-six miles in one stretch, and there was the danger that something could slow us down—for instance, a fallen tree blocking the river—and we'd either be unable to get back or get back so late that it would be dark. I wasn't quite ready to paddle the Ocklawaha at night, but Bob had already tested his new flashlight to see how long it would keep a charge. In retrospect, this line of reasoning was preposterous, but at the time, I didn't know any better. It got worse.

"If it rains," Bob said, darkly, "there could be flash floods. Our kayaks are flimsy. It could be dangerous."

"Oh well," I said. Flash floods were a bit of a stretch to think of, even for someone from a mountainous area. I wanted to remind him that this was just north of central Florida, which seldom has problems with flash flooding. Instead, I tried a bit of bravado and said, "We're in our sixties, after all. We can't live forever."

Bob looked at me. "Well?" I said. "I mean, if there was ever a time of life when you shouldn't let your fears hold you back, it's now."

"Maybe," Bob said. "Maybe we should see if there are any tours left on the river." He said the word "tours" as if his mouth contained a bitter pill.

"Not a chance. That would be cheating." I was baiting him.

"Perhaps," Bob replied. "But at least it will keep me from having rotator cuff surgery."

Bob, the family pragmatist, who was ready to paddle an unfamiliar river twenty-six miles in the dark, was thinking of the out-of-pocket insurance deductible. I pretended to concede. "Maybe you do have a point." It seemed my remarks had their intended effect.

By scouting the internet, I found an ad for a place on the fringe of the Ocala National Forest run by a guy named Mike O'Neal, who went to Ocala High School and was "still doing this." By "this," he meant renting out canoes and kayaks from Eureka and driving paddlers to Gores Landing, where they could kayak downstream back to Eureka. His business, which he ran with his wife, Sheri, was called Ocklawaha Canoe Outpost and Resort, which covered about seven and a half acres with waterfront access to the Ocklawaha River.

So, instead of paddling twenty-six miles, some of it under the stars, we planned to paddle nine miles downstream in broad daylight. When we got to his camp at about 9:15 on Sunday morning, Mike told us about spots along the river where we could set up a tent on the raw shoreline, build a fire and stay the night. I was all for it, although Bob gave a definitive no on account of ticks, which love him and have burrowed into some inopportune spots neither he nor I will ever forget.

Still, I was elated at how all this was working out. True, we would be going north and miss paddling the miles between our beachy bluff five miles downstream from Ray Wayside Park to Gores Landing, but we could make that up another time. And, in addition to offering a safer, less strenuous trip,

Mike's outpost also rented out cabins for overnight stays. They were prefab units, about two hundred to four hundred square feet, with porches and a clean kitchen lined with shelves and a bedroom with bunks on either side of the wall. Out front were a picnic table and a charcoal grill.

"I could live here," I said.

Of course, coming back was all contingent upon us finishing our trips before the summer was upon us. As Mike said, "It's so hot here then, your eyeballs sweat."

As Mike drove us and our gear from the outpost to Gores Landing, he also threw cold water on our idea to paddle the Ocklawaha as far as Palatka. "Too much 'lettuce' in the water," he said:

> Look, I'm practically the only independent guy on the river. The rest is all water agencies. The Army Corps of Engineers, the St. Johns River Water Management District, Florida Fish and Wildlife Conservation Commission, Marion County Soil and Water Commission. What no one seems to understand is that the water is so much lower than it used to be. In Florida, water is more valuable than oil.

The Gores Landing unit of the Ocklawaha River consists of almost three thousand acres along the Ocklawaha between Gores Landing and County Road 316. The launch we went to is actually in Fort McCoy, which is in northeast Marion County. Three other cars, laden with canoes and motorboats and kayaks, pulled up while Mike and Bob unloaded the red tandem Old Town Loon kayak. We put our cooler and Bob's cameras, tripod and fishing poles in the sixteen-foot boat and said goodbye to Mike.

"See you in four or five hours," he said. "You guys are experienced, right? You know what you're doing?"

Bob and I looked at each other. Then we looked at Mike. We nodded.

"What about the alligators?" I asked.

"Water's still cold." Mike said. "They won't be hungry for another month."

"Great news," I said.

Mike said, "But don't go into any of the tributaries. Because all the noise and commotion on the river drives the fish over there. And the snakes." He grinned. "If you're not back at 5:00 [p.m.], we start worrying. If you're not back by six, we go out in the boat looking for you. But if you're in one of the tributaries, we are not gonna know where to look."

"OK," Bob said.

The red double kayak with the flat bottom easily accommodated our swag. We waved to Mike and pushed off, me in the front, Bob in the back. The kayak was comfortable, but we'd left our coats in the car, and it was cooler and windier than we thought. The breezes were stiff, ruffling the water and chilling us. Still, we were sure four hours of paddling would warm us up.

I dipped my hand over the side, and the water of the river was cold and clear as a cube of ice. We could see to the bottom, but unlike on our other two trips down the Ocklawaha, there was no eel grass, no fish and nary a bird call. It reminded me of other hikes we'd made on "bird" trails in Florida, where all we saw were wolf spiders and dung beetles. The water bugs skittered over the surface of the Ocklawaha, but there was no other sign of life. The only people we saw were secluded and half-hidden by trees, fishing from johnboats in the tributaries Mike had warned us about.

"Will we see manatees?" I asked Bob.

"Not a chance."

I looked up. Bob said, "You have this big reservoir, and manatees have to find this one little channel outlet. The odds are against it." He was silent for a minute. "Did people used to eat manatees?"

"Ugh," I said. "But I guess. They weigh over a thousand pounds."

We passed beachfront campsites with blackened campfires. We got out at one and looked around. We had to climb a sandy bluff, and there was a trail leading back into the woods, which I decided would be unbearable in the summer with the heat and mosquitos. At this time of year, the only sign of life was a single monarch butterfly. We had seen yellow acres of milkweed along the banks. In a week or so, there would probably be butterflies everywhere.

Two huge great blue herons flew over our heads, and we passed a flock of black buzzards feasting on what smelled like rotten fish. Mike had given us a map with the stops along the river: Piney landing, boat ramp, Sunday Bluff. Each had a charred campsite, although we didn't see any trash.

We did see our first monkey about three and a half miles into the trip. He was small and brown with a furry muff around his wizened face—maybe a rhesus. He was up in the ragged top of a cabbage palm, and when he saw us, he skittered down and disappeared among the scrub. Bob imagined he followed us for the rest of the trip, making monkey sounds along the banks, but I didn't see him again.

Monkeys are not considered a feral species on the river; they were always considered more of a tourist attraction. Some people say that the original nine

Left: Picture of Highway 316 bridge over Ocklawaha River in Eureka in 1965. *Florida Memories*.

Below: Present-day Highway 316 bridge.

monkeys arrived in Silver Springs in the 1930s for the Johnny Weissmuller Tarzan movies. Other people say that the monkeys were released by a steamboat captain in the 1920s in Silver River State Park. Either way, it was a long time ago, and the original few monkeys have grown to an estimated one thousand rhesus monkeys living in the nearby wetlands. Since they can swim, some show up in Ocala, Jacksonville and Sarasota. They should not be fed, and they do carry human diseases—the herpes B virus, for example.

Concrete disc that acted as a drawbridge.

We passed the boat ramp, where someone was fishing. Bob's line had broken early in the trip. He called, "Doing any good?" The guy shook his head. At that point, I had never seen anyone catch a fish on the Ocklawaha River. I knew people who fished—both Bob and our daughter Corrie did it, and so did numerous friends. Where were the fish stories, the tales of catching fifty bass an hour? Were Ocklawaha River fisherman just abnormally modest?

I would have to wait to find out.

We made good time, even with stopping twice. Soon, the Highway 316 bridge, which was supposed to mark the Cross-Florida Barge Canal, loomed into view. We were about twenty miles south of the Rodman dam. Some guy with a white beard was standing on his open truck bed smoking a cigarette. We just drifted in and looked up at the underside of the bridge as a car or two rumbled overhead. We saw nothing but mud daubers and wasp nests.

Ahead was a large round concrete object—mired in the river, now obsolete—that Bob speculated was used to rotate and open an old drawbridge.

We scraped the hull of the kayak on the shallow beach of the outpost landing. Gingerly, we climbed out, threw the oars and lifejackets in the kayak seats and walked up the short, grassy incline. Then, we stood outside Mike's stilt house and hollered that we were back. He showed us his scrapbooks before we left and told us about a pontoon boat on the other side steered by Captain Erika, who "has lived on the river forever."

I imagined that would be a fun time, and maybe our next trip—but I was wrong.

4

RODMAN DAM LOOP

May 13, 2017

*Below Eureka lies a graphic history of how the wildest river
can be broken and put between shafts.*
—*Paul Brooks*

Early in the morning, Bob, Jack Bass and I took the canoe to a launch behind Rodman dam and paddled a three-mile loop down the manmade canal portion of the Cross-Florida Barge Canal on the east side of Rodman Lake. It was a two-hour drive to get there under a starry sky and through a hidden haze over the landscape that emerged slowly as the sun rose. It seems when you get out into nature there is always a mist, which gradually clears, and then the wildlife emerges.

We saw wild turkeys feeding on the side of the road, sleek and brown with prim beaks and beady eyes.

I never drive to these excursions; I'm always the passenger, sitting in the middle of the truck's cab, and it has occurred to me more than once that I would be hard-pressed to find any of these launches on my own. We've been to at least four now, and although the landmarks are familiar to me, the way to them is not.

Still, I was cheered as we went over a bridge, and I saw the sign: Ocklawaha River. Jack, who must know every launch in Florida, drove into a small paved lot behind the dam. It had a picturesque sandy push-off point and, early as it was, two people were already out there sitting in canvas chairs with fishing poles in their hands and a Styrofoam ice bucket at their feet. Even if, at that point, I had never seen anyone catch a fish on the Ocklawaha, it was reassuring to me that no matter what happens in Florida, the fishing capital of the world, millions of people all over the state are willing to get up early, grab a fishing pole and sit by the banks of some river, or on a bridge, and steadily watch the line they've cast in the water.

The men asked, "Are you doing any good?" The strangers shook their heads and smiled. Bob and Jack brought their own lines and lures, too, which they stuffed into the canoe along with the cooler, life-preservers and paddles. I wore a brown belly pack that I've had since the 1980s. Ziplocked into plastic bags inside were my sunglasses, one ten-dollar bill and one one-dollar bill, Chapstick, tissues, my mobile phone and crackers. We typically go lean on a day excursion, but it occurred to me that I should start bringing a compass. Jack warned us about water moccasins, and there was a sign near the restroom advertising the presence of venomous snakes.

Jack climbed in the back, I got in the middle and Bob pushed us off and hopped in the front. We were careful to keep our gravity centered lest we have an early morning baptism, and none of us were foot-washers. The water was low and clear. We could see pebbles and bottle caps on the sandy floor of the river. There was the sound of birds and the sound of water. The thin layer of mist stirred as though the river was breathing.

Jack said, "I don't care what's happening, when I'm on the river, I'm happy."

Around the time the Ocklawaha was dammed, Jack's grandfather sold his camp:

> *I thought he got rid of it because of the overhunting of the forest; the game wasn't like it was when he first was there. Then there was deer, bear, and turkey—everything that a woodsman would want. Over the years, it just kind of got depleted. It used to be like the wild west, poachers everywhere. I thought that was why he left. But Grandma said, "No, it was because of the dammed river. I know he loved the river."*

We paddled past the back of the dam, a big gray fortress. To educate myself, I'd joined a Facebook group called Restore the Ocklawaha. The group is rife with pictures and articles such as, "Dams be Damned, Let the World's Rivers Flow Again." Despite federal money allocated for river restoration in the 1970s, the Rodman dam remains, its reservoir, or "pool," now used only as a bass fishing basin. The dam impounds water in a pool, and whatever flows down the river into the dam flows through the spillway of the dam and on down to the St. Johns. It is rumored that manatees get trapped in there. One Ocklawahan posted:

> *I see more manatees moving into Silver Springs during the winter if the Ocklawaha River was reconnected. Then, they could navigate freely rather than happen to make their way through Buckman Locks occasionally like they do now.*

Anglers who fish the Rodman Reservoir dispute this. On their "Save Rodman Dam" website, they counter that hundreds of manatees safely pass through the locks. Jim Gross, executive director of the nonprofit organization Florida Defenders of the Environment, says the state has made the dam and lock "somewhat safer" for manatees compared to earlier times. Still, manatee sightings are rare upstream of the dam.

In addition to the manatees, environmentalists and riverkeepers worry about the water quality and quantity. More evaporation of water in the reservoir means less overall flow for the river. The Sierra Club states that "the historic flow rates of Silver Springs have declined dramatically...the springs and the Silver River are suffering from excessive nitrate levels."

I cast a proprietary eye about me, scanning for algae blooms or other toxic signs of deterioration. I saw none. I did see acres of water hyacinths (*Eichhornia crassipes*), which are deemed a nuisance and an infestation by the U.S. Army Corps of Engineers. In the nineteenth century, a snowbird near Palatka, in a misguided attempt at landscaping, hosted water hyacinths in her backyard, which happened to be on the St. Johns River. Within a decade, the flowery hyacinths covered fifty million acres of the river. They are almost impossible to eradicate.

In the 1950s, the herbicide 2,4-D (Dichlorophenoxyacetic acid) was found to be effective killing hyacinth. When funding trickled off in 1996, the Senate made a five-million-dollar appropriation to the APC (Aquatic Plant Control). By 1999, a federal invasive species counsel was organized. Despite all of that poison, the Army Corps of Engineers states on their website that "water hyacinth now infests all of the Gulf Coast states and continues into the Carolinas."

The fight between man and nature isn't cheap. The Invasive Plant Management section of the Florida Fish and Wildlife Conservation Commission has spent an average of $10,000 annually on the Upper Ocklawaha River and an average of $3,019 annually from Silver River to Eureka. Diquat, an industrial aquatic weed-killer, is the primary herbicide used on the river. In a special report published by the St. Johns River Water Management district in 2010, the agency had this to say about the poison:

> *Currently…contact herbicides registered by the U.S. Environmental Protection Agency (EPA) for hydrilla use in Florida waters: copper, diquat dibromide, and endothall. Copper compounds are rarely approved by the FWC for use in Florida public waters. Diquat dibromide causes severe necrosis of hydrilla 14 to 21 days after application but it is rapidly adsorbed to organic and clay particles and is therefore a less desirable option in the turbid waters of the Ocklawaha Chain of Lakes.*

Still, some scientists claim water hyacinths can provide a habitable environment for fish and wildlife. Largemouth bass gorge on crayfish that hide amongst their fine, feathery roots. Their glossy green leaves and bulbous stalks, tipped with rich purple flowers, and their hanging roots sift algae and help prevent nitration. Manatees eat them. We could eat them, too, if we wanted to soak and cook them to take away their fiery tang. They blanket portions of the water like floating versions of flowering mangroves. They are a nuisance, but they are pretty. As Floridians, we know well enough that invasive plants and vines show up everywhere on water as well as on land.

But the question remained: What was Rodman Lake—a nutrient sink or a filter?

It seems to depend upon whose side you might be on—the bass fishing enthusiasts and elected officials or colleges, nonprofits, environmentalists and local people who grew up on the river.

Concerning the former, Putnam County commissioner Larry Harvey, a self-professed environmentalist, states unequivocally that the dam should stay because "it filters the nitrates going into the St. Johns River…kind of like a kidney cleans out before waste leaves the body."

The reservoir (called Lake Ocklawaha by its proponents) is ranked by the Save Rodman Dam proponents as one of the finest bass fishing locales in the United States. Anglers catch record breaking fourteen-pound largemouth bass in tournaments, mostly on the reservoir, improving its national reputation and stature. The tournaments bring tourists to Marion and Putnam Counties, and proponents of the dam worry about losing that economic boost. Although a 2016 study by the University of Florida proves that more people come to the river for recreation than anglers come to the reservoir to fish, the Rodman dam proponents think they should have it all.

They have their talking points. They argue that the reservoir is a reserve of drinking water if the Florida aquifer runs dry. Yet, according to a 2005 Ocklawaha River water allocation study by the St. Johns River Water Management District, it is impossible to manage the pool as a drinking water reservoir and simultaneously manage the fishery:

> [I]t appears that if maintaining Rodman Reservoir as a viable recreational sport fishery and aquatic ecosystem is the management objective, then more water may be available from the river system under the Full Restoration-2010 management alternative than would be available if the reservoir is retained.

Additionally, and paradoxically, if water supply is a concern, it is a mystery why, in 2018, the St. Johns River Water Management District allowed a Canadian billionaire, Frank Stronach, to pump 1.1 million gallons per day out of an aquifer near Silver Springs to run a cattle ranch.

There are even theories that special interests are behind the breaching of the dam to increase water flow and deepen the Port of Jacksonville for larger commercial cargo vessels. On the Jaxport webpage, the agency admits that "deepening the harbor is essential to meet the needs of larger cargo ships transiting the Suez and Panama Canals as those vessels deliver cargo to JAXPORT terminals." But according to news reports, it is not environmentalists but the Jacksonville business community and the Florida Department of Transportation who are pushing to deepen the harbor. In fact, an editorial in the *Florida Times-Union* stated, "An earlier proposal to support opening the Rodman dam and infusing fresh water into the St. Johns River ran into a hurricane of political opposition from Putnam County."

Still, the Save Rodman Dam proponents clearly have the upper hand. According to Jim Gross, "They have what they want, and they don't seem interested in talking about the restoration issue."

Yet many studies, both recent and older, support breaching the dam. A 2016 technical publication studying the effects from the restoration of the Ocklawaha River and created by the St. Johns River Water Management district, a neutral agency, stated: "The positive aspects related to the restoration of floodplain functions, increased unique habitat and migratory fish passage appeared to provide overall net environmental gain." And, according to a 2015 study by Dr. Chris Hendrickson, a Hamerschlag University professor of engineering and an expert on inland waterways, "a free-flowing river that has no Rodman pool would add to the spring flow and create two healthier rivers: the Ocklawaha and the St. Johns." Other people who ought to know, such as the St. Johns Riverkeeper, Lisa Rinaman, unequivocally state that "breaching of the dam is the critical restoration project for Northeast Florida."

Bob, Jack and I had fallen silent. On that day, the sun never emerged, and the sky looked the color of iron. A long cable connected with flat round buoys separates the dam from the river. On each buoy was a cormorant. Some spread their wings to dry. It occurred to me that instead of chasing wildlife out of their natural habitat, the dam forced wildlife to adapt to it. Manatees would undoubtedly benefit from a free-flowing Ocklawaha, as would black bears, indigo snakes and several plant species. There has been a documented decrease in plant and animal diversity since the creation of the reservoir because of upland flooding.

I know the river can never return to what it was. But I wonder if, someday, it could *resemble* what it was. Then, I remember seeing the fishermen at Rodman dam earlier this morning and wonder what they think. How will it affect them? They have a bigger stake in these waters than most. According to some game wardens, anglers are subsistence fishermen who can barely scrape up enough money to buy the gas to get them to the dam to catch fish for their dinner that night. I look into the water and see a good-sized soft-shell turtle swim by in the clear water.

"There's huge gar in the river," Jack said. "And mullet. There used to be huge catfish. Catfish as big as a small child. There were stingrays. They call them skates. You still have those up in the Wekiva." I know from my readings that the St. Johns is solid with skates. However, for some reason, you don't find them much in the Ocklawaha. Jack is a natural raconteur, and like most raconteurs, he does stretch the fish story a tad.

Jack went on:

> *My grandfather and my uncle and I were going down the river in a canoe; it was only a two-seater, I was sitting in the bottom, and I saw something coming toward us. It looked like a submarine. We were heading west, and it was heading east. It was as long, or damn near as long as our canoe, which would have been sixteen feet long.*

Bob said, "What? Did you see the Loch Ness [monster]?"
Jack shook his head:

It was an alligator gar. The water was so shallow it couldn't submerge itself. You could see its eyes, its fin and its tail as it was making its way through there. It was the biggest fish I've ever seen in my life. It was a monster. Its eyes were as big around as a Coke can.

I looked around warily and started as fish leapt out of the water in exuberant splashes. We paddled past the barge canal and back on to the river channel. The water was stagnant, with ominous little bubbles on the surface. Jack explained about drawdowns and how they work,

"The last time they drew down was in 2015," Jack said. He was right. Later, I looked it up on the Florida Fish and Wildlife Conservation Commission's website:

When the Rodman Reservoir drawdown is underway, waters stay down until the spring of 2016. The reservoir will be seven feet below normal water level for over three months from the middle of November 2015 to the beginning of March 2016.

Some people say the reservoir is already so shallow it should be called a pool. During the drawdown, when the gates are opened on the impoundment and the river flows freely, people flock to the river. Lost springs bubble. There is hope that if the dam is ever breached, the influx of manatees alone would increase tourism. After all, only slightly northwest of the peninsula is Crystal River, where tourists flock from all over the globe to see hundreds of manatees in the winter. In 2017, a University of Florida study determined that a free-flowing Ocklawaha River would nearly double economic opportunity in Marion and Putnam Counties by boosting tourism, enabling people to spend time and money on the river, fishing, camping, kayaking and bird-watching. The same study stated that more tourists showed up for these activities on the river—and spent more money—than tourists to the Rodman Reservoir.

There are many economically and ecologically sound alternatives to the Rodman dam. Some state agencies float the idea of adopting a registration fee for kayaks, canoes and paddleboats to generate revenue for state waters—revenue that could replace the money that comes from the reservoir tournaments. There is the Silver Ocklawaha Blueway Action Plan, sponsored by river advocates, which could open an aquatic trail between the Silver and Ocklawaha Rivers, leaving the dam untouched.

A river—any river—is, among other things, a political point of contention, and the Ocklawaha is no exception. In fact, the river represents

Snowy egrets and ibis at the Rodman dam.

the longest-running environmental battle in Florida. It was hard for us to believe, from our vantage of the river, that the reality of our present surroundings was jeopardized in any way or that the river would not always be there. Yet its fate depended, as it always has, on elected officials, the courts and environmental activists.

That day, the water on the Ocklawaha River was very low. There were no trap markers, but there were orange strings attached to "bush hooks" on low-lying branches set to catch catfish and turtles or even gators. These are illegal if baited with freshwater game fish like bream (also known as bluegill), which attract the big cats at night. We saw a large gator lurking at eye level near the bank, but he submerged as we passed him.

Jack said:

> *One day, I was with my grandma, and there was a little squirrel running up and down the cypress tree. Out of the blue, this alligator's tail came out of the water and hit that cypress tree so hard it knocked bark off. I learned right there—that alligator, if he wanted to, could knock you out of a boat using his tail as a bullwhip.*

Sunning Silver
River cooter.

Bob and Jack cast their lines. Jack said, "You want to cast toward the trees and draw in slowly." The men tried this for a while. Despite the leaping fish, there were no bites, and Bob broke his line twice. If it were me, I would have given up already. But Bob was used to casting on open waters, and he found the tight quarters challenging.

We paddled on, following the winding path of the river. We saw drops flattening the river surface and felt a little moisture on our faces. Jack's wife, Darlene, called and said a storm front was approaching through Ocala. "Well, it's too late now," Jack said.

Around the next bend, we heard a God-awful racket. I strained to see and finally noticed flashes of feathers and wings thrashing around inside a pair of sweetgum trees. Unbelievably, a red-shouldered hawk had attacked two wood ducks and a wild turkey amidst the great squawking. Our appearance probably disorientated the giant bird, which flew off. The wood ducks escaped, and the turkey, stupidly, retreated to the tree where the hawk originally perched. The hawk flew off and circled over our heads, perhaps in search of the ducks. We watched the turkey for a while as it hid under the tree beyond the yellow buds of spatterdock. He kept venturing out and then retreating. I've heard that turkey hunters spend a lot of money to buy expensive camouflage, face paint, guns and calls. They say these birds are wily and difficult to kill…I'm not so sure.

We moved on through a light drizzle. We saw limpkins in the marsh and great herons fly over our heads with their vast wings flapping. Jack pointed out an osprey. I have trouble telling them apart from buzzards. Jack explained that ospreys tend to be lighter in color with a narrower wing span.

It was a shorter loop than we'd anticipated, and before we knew it, we were rounding the bend toward the launch, and the same two people were sitting on the banks with their lines in the water and a catfish in their cooler. Finally, someone caught a fish. We loaded up the canoe and gear in Jack's truck and talked desolately of finding another launch, but the sky was still steel gray and piling on some rain-laden clouds. Darlene sent me a worried text about the approaching storm.

So, in the end, we went back to Rodman dam, found our footing on the concrete slope and stared down at the water, which gushed through the gates and sent islands of foam floating down the canal. There, set amid logs of wood, concrete slabs and greenery where cowbirds stalk tiny crabs, the dam loomed.

The Rodman dam is twenty-two feet high and close to seven thousand feet long with a concrete spillway and four gates, which control the water level of the reservoir. There is no way around it—the dam is an unnatural chunk of earth, an eyesore, a medieval fortress. People say the dam is leaking and the metal parts look rusty. People thought that a new spring had developed, but the water was really leaking out of the dam and percolating up. The cost to repair the leak is prohibitive. There is a standoff between the dam proponents and opponents. Nature and time will decide its fate.

That day, many people had their lines in the water, and I finally saw some real fishing action: Shore fishers and boat fishers. Men and women sat on coolers on the sides of the banks or a pier, poles in the water, orange buckets full of bream topped with bags of ice. Parallel were the anglers dangling their long fly lines with four-pound monofilament from fancy bass fishing boats.

A day of fishing
at Rodman dam.

I have heard there are times when the fish bite well, and when they do, a kind of ESP is transmitted to anglers loud and clear. In the spring, the perimeter of the Rodman dam fills up, and the pole lines are two feet across. Bass, bream and catfish are full into their spawn. By late summer, the bulk of the catfish leave and return to the St. Johns River.

When the bass bite, there are cries of "whee-ha" when a lucky angler, wearing neon orange or green, reels in his catch and says, "All I need is one more bass to give ta my boy."

If you hang around long enough, you see some flouting of the law. An angler may surreptitiously measure the fish and slip it into a friend's bucket; the limit is five largemouth bass per person per day, and only one may be sixteen inches or longer in total length.

A nagging thought returned to me: "If the dam goes away, what will happen to the people who fish the reservoir to put food on their table?" Most people say they'll just learn to fish another way. Local people say the biggest bass caught at the tournament last spring was not from the reservoir.

Down by the banks littered with broken chunks of concrete, a family of otters swam, their sleek, dark heads bobbing above and below the surface of the water. They climbed onto the artificial embankment—wet,

Family of otters near Rodman dam.

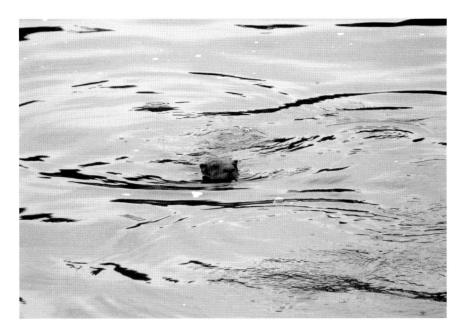

Swimming otter near Rodman dam.

black and awkward. It was a mother and four babies. Nearby, a buzzard ominously flapped its wings. The mother otter led her family into the brush, and the buzzard hopped after them. But buzzards only eat dead food, right? Jack explained that they're there for the scraps of bait and fish left by the bank fishermen.

Against all odds, nature appears to be thriving above, on and around the controversial dam that sits like a scar on the waterway. There is no stopping something wild.

5

A CRUISING DOWN THE RIVER

June 24, 2017

Nature, Mr. Allnut, is what we are put in this world to rise above.
—Rose Sayer (Katharine Hepburn) to Charlie Allnut (Humphrey Bogart)
in The African Queen

When one goes to Europe, one visits ancient castles. When one goes to Florida, one visits ancient rivers. Captain Erika Ritter runs a boat tour in her pontoon boat, *The Anhinga Spirit*, off the Eureka West Boat Ramp on Highway 316 east of Fort McCoy and Highway 315. I got her business card off the counter of Mike O'Neal's Ocklawaha Canoe Outpost and Resort. An eco-tour trip with Captain Erika entailed a full history of the past and present of the Ocklawaha River. On her website, Captain Erika writes:

> *My name is Captain Erika. I am a native of Florida. As the saying goes "I have sand in my shoes." Since the early 1800's my family has been in Florida. I have been fishin on the river since I was 3 years old. I love it so much I started a pontoon boat business on the great and famous Ocklawaha River. My first vessel was a canoe at age 17.*

Bob and I took two and a half hours and had a little trouble finding the Eureka West Boat Ramp in the Ocala National Forest, mainly because there is no phone or internet service out there, and like so many people without GPS, we are lost in our natural environment. We went north and south a few times and ended up in someone's yard—the someone being a thirtyish homeowner with a furiously barking dog that flung itself against the wire fence so violently that his owner's directions were, by necessity, mostly gestures. As we turned to leave, I had a new appreciation for what Darwin so aptly described as survival of the fittest. And for the briefest of moments, I imagined the monstrous canine, with its glowering eyes and popping, saliva-laden jaws, bounding over the fence and upon us. Bob and I were happy to once again be safely ensconced in our vehicle.

Despite our early start, we ended up barely making the agreed upon 10:00 a.m. launch time. Bob and I pulled up in a nearby dirt parking lot, parked next to a camper and hurried to the boat ramp. We saw another couple standing in a pontoon boat. They looked like part of the landscape, as though they had always been there and always would be.

Captain Erika was a middle-aged woman with graying hair. She had a petite build and was tidy in appearance, wearing denim blue capris, sunglasses on a lanyard and a white button-down blouse. She called out in a resonant voice, "Are you Liz?"

"Yes," I said. "And this is my husband, Bob."

"Welcome aboard, Bob."

Captain Erika described her boat as a "a sturdy 1990 Flote Bote powered by a 2006 four-stroke Nissan outboard." It was roomy and had a stable platform that could safely accommodate an entire family.

Bob teased, as he came aboard, "Where's my life vest?"

Erika laughed and introduced us to her neighbor, Richard, a stocky, white-haired chap who was slouched in one of the three chairs on the deck. He was coming along for the three-hour tour up and down the Ocklawaha River.

It was already hot outside, and Bob's backpack was loaded with sunblock, but the visor shade of the canvas T-top offered protection from the sun. The water was full of hyacinths, and Erika said the water was "high." I had to do some research to find out what this meant.

A river's flow cycles consist of periods of higher water levels when the river accumulates waste. At lower levels, the accumulated debris dries up and blows away. However, the Rodman dam sits between the Ocklawaha and St. Johns Rivers, and it is the largest influence in the elevation of the Ocklawaha River. According to Jim Gross, executive director of the Florida Defenders of the Environment (FDE), "The natural rhythm of the river has been disturbed by the dam."

Gross referred me to Thomas Crisman, a professor in the School of Geosciences at the University of South Florida, who confirmed his remarks. According to Dr. Crisman, "Dams regulate downstream flow by holding back water and releasing it at more predictable rates. Instead of the river experiencing cycles of up and down depending on upstream water sources, the dam smooths out the flow to a point where it can be held at a relatively constant rate."

When the Rodman reservoir is lowered during drawdowns to clean out plant life in the pool, suppressed springs (the lost springs) start to flow. Thinking about the lost springs—which, at that point, I knew little about—reminded me of something.

I asked Erika, "Were you at the Matheson Museum last night?"

She had sent me an email the day before: "Not sure if you can attend but there is a showing of the Lost Springs film of the Ocklawaha in Gainesville 6:00 tonight at the Matheson History Museum. 513 East University Ave."

"Oh yeah," she said. "I was part of that whole process. I was one of the first captains taking them out there and showing them the springs."

"How many are there?"

"Springs? Over twenty."

Lost Springs is a documentary film about a collection of freshwater Florida springs that are suppressed because of the Rodman dam. Bob and I were going to see it in Jacksonville at the Museum of Contemporary Art (MOCA) in September. Captain Erika said the springs were "lost" because of the weight of the water flooded by the impounded river.

Captain Erika took a minute to pull out a map. She laid it across the hood and aligned it so the top faced north. Then, she purposefully planted one finger on a spot on a narrow bend near Eureka and explained, "We're here and going north," she said. "I want you to see how the river looks natural, and this," she pointed, "is where they stopped the barge canal."

"What is the goal of environmental activists now?" I asked. "The government stopped the construction on the barge canal; they'll never start it again. What do they want to do about Rodman dam?" I already kind of knew the answer to that question from perusing Captain Erika's website. But I wanted to hear it from her.

"They wanna breach it," Captain Erika said. "So we get the fish and the flow levels properly back in there. That's mandated."

Political pressure from environmental activists led by Marjorie Harris Carr caused President Richard Nixon to permanently suspend construction on the Cross-Florida Barge Canal in 1971. Could a similar campaign finally eradicate Rodman dam? The purists, such as Captain Erika, wish to return all lands and waters razed by the U.S. Army Corps of Engineers to their natural habitats. The Ocklawaha wouldn't be the first river that had to be put back to how it was. The Kissimmee River, in south central Florida, is an excellent example. According to a 2016 article in *National Geographic*, Washington's Elwha River "has been thriving since the removal of its hydroelectric dam system....Some hope that the restoration of the Elwha River will become a shining example for the removal of dams across the U.S."

Still, there was an unanswered million-dollar question.

"Why hasn't it ever been done?" I asked.

"The EPA [Environmental Protection Agency] doesn't take it seriously. It is a nasty political boondoggle," Captain Erika said. "Upstream of the dam? Down in the Rodman pool, all it does is generate rotted plant vegetation. And fish kills, a horrible dying thing. The Eureka dam stops right here at the tree line?" She pointed to the map. A tree line, found at high elevations, is the edge of the environment at which trees can grow. From the Eureka County Road 316 Bridge upstream to the junction with the Silver River near State Route 40, the floodplain trees are in excellent condition. Yet, from the Eureka County Road 316 Bridge downstream to the area near Cannon Springs, the trees are stressed from the backwater impact of the Rodman dam. Downstream from the Cannon Springs area, most of the native floodplain trees left standing have already drowned. They are floating hulks and hazards to river navigation.

Captain Erika continued:

> *The downhill side where the river wants to be is over on the east side. Any time you stop high waters full of nutrients, the dissolved oxygen is absorbed on sunny days by algae blooms going crazy. And then the fish can't breathe. Eels, all kinds of stuff drown.*

She shook her head and said:

> *First, they [the water district] had to establish flow levels. Which they just did. Everybody is freaking out over that because they just established an acceptable flow from Silver River's all-time low. In 2018, they have to renew these permits for flooding and draining. So, the permit to flood Rodman pool, and keep it flooded—which is illegal—a judge extended it for more studies.*

Around us were the sounds of birds and gently lapping water. Far off in the distance was the strain of a motorboat. Erika continued: "The St.

Johns River is highly polluted. Every day, they herbicide that river of plants that give shade, free-floating water lettuce [*Pistia spathulata*] and hyacinth. It's money for chemical companies. Our tax dollars pay them."

I mulled this over. I have heard fish stories from anglers about catching their limit of largemouth bass ten days running, so, struggling or not, the St. Johns River is not yet dead from pollution. Captain Erika is, of course, correct—to a degree. The St. Johns is not the river it was two hundred years ago. One of the problems is the drawing out of potable water upstream, from Sanford into the St. Johns. If it continues, it's clear the St. Johns will become nothing more than a tidal lagoon. In fact, according to a local game warden, there was a six-week period in 2017 (before Hurricane Irma) when there was no outgoing tide in the St. Johns.

Erika laughed, bitterly, and I looked up from my musing. "When I was a kid, they did not allow herbicides. The first ones caused massive death. Everything died."

I asked, "Doesn't the hyacinth block the river and get into boat motors?" Even in 1896, growths of hyacinths in the St. Johns River were responsible for navigational hazards and kept steamboats from reaching their docks in Palatka. They often stranded fishermen until the water weeds were blown apart by wind. Hyacinth growth can push riverboats out of the main channel.

Erika said, "They could maintain it at a certain level, and they could do mechanical harvesting."

Mechanical harvesting is what "Colonel" Hubbard Hart was contracted to do on the Ocklawaha River in 1865. The government paid him $4,500 to clear the Ocklawaha from Palatka to Silver Springs, which had never before been attempted. It took Hart two years to remove 300 trees and 172 logs from the bottom of the river. The "floating islands" of water lettuce had to be "sawed in pieces and the fragments suffered to float down or fastened to shore."

"Mechanical harvesting is not a cancer-causing fallout chemical," Erika said. "And they've added two more chemicals recently."

"Do you know the names of the chemicals?" A local man told us that he thinks sometimes "instead of spraying, they just dump the chemicals in one spot and they're done with it." As far back as the 1960s, Rachel Carson stated in *Silent Spring*: "Chemical pollution is the third-ranking cause of species extinction in the United States, after habitat destruction and biological pollution."

Captain Erika said, "There's a list of them when they send you the spray notices? It's [an herbicide], it's all these different things."

Aquatic Plant Control (APC) has been practiced around the rivers in Florida and other southern states for a long time. In 1899, Congress authorized the River and Harbor Act and the amount of $36,000 for the removal of the hyacinths. The Secretary of War, Russell A. Alger, used his own discretion in the removal, employing both mechanical and chemical means.

One of the more popular herbicides, invented in 1974, contains glyphosate, a broad-spectrum systemic herbicide. It is the second–most popular poison behind 2,4-D. It kills living plants after being absorbed through their foliage and produces herbicide-resistant vegetation, causing "super or noxious weeds." There is speculation that it is also cancer-causing, particularly regarding non-Hodgkin's lymphoma. Toxicology reviews by the International Agency for Research on Cancer in 2013 and 2014 concluded that glyphosate was "probably" carcinogenic to humans. Although it has been banned in five countries, recent studies by the EPA stated that cancer-causing levels of glyphosate in the environment are too low to cause actual harm.

Still, why would anyone want to keep the Rodman dam intact when the result is stagnant river flow levels, the need to use herbicides and algae blooms on the pristine waters?

Bob asked, "Does the bass fishing community want to keep the pool behind Rodman dam?"

Captain Erika shrugged. "A lot of the stock was killed in the fish kills." She's right about that. According to a final environmental impact statement put out by the U.S. Department of Agriculture and the Southern Region Forest Service in 2001, at least 11 million fish have died in the reservoir zone.

She is also backed up by author Leroy Wight, who, in 2006, wrote this in *Saving the St. Johns River*: "The expensive effort to maintain Rodman as a fishery has lasted over two decades at a cost approaching $20 million. Part of the difficulty lies in the fact that Rodman is not a true reservoir but merely…a shallow weed-filled backwater spread over the original flood plain…subject to massive fish-kills and beset with submerged logs."

Still, according to adamant local citizens, the dam offers some of the best bass fishing around. The Florida Fish and Wildlife Conservation Commission contends that the reservoir and the river "offer great fishing opportunities." They don't stock the Ocklawaha River or the reservoir because "fishing is in good shape."

The annual tournaments are a huge selling point for Putnam County tourism. Those who express their affinity for maintaining the dam have good intentions that are usually economic. Part of the discussion that environmental activists were trying to start with the "Save Rodman Dam" proponents had to do with finding other avenues to boost tourism in Putnam County.

Erika squinted into the sun. She seemed to be collecting her thoughts. Perhaps she was thinking of the sacrifice of a free-flowing river to provide fishing in a limited area to reservoir fans. She jabbed her finger toward the east, beyond the earthen berm and concrete dam, and said, "The St. Johns River is right there. That's where the big fish are. The St. Johns River—that's where the striped bass are, that's where the shrimp are." I remember that the Ocklawaha is the largest tributary to the St. Johns.

"Not the pool?" I wondered how this could be if so many trophy largemouth bass are caught by recreational anglers and professional bass fishermen.

"What would be a benefit is twenty springs for you to paddle to. We say this is the tourist attraction. Every study has shown—by all environmental agencies, not just the radical environmental groups—the EPA, they say, 'Get rid of the dam.'"

"Then, would the fish come back?"

Captain Erika said, "There's no striped bass in this river anymore. The eels are practically gone. The eels were bass food. Years ago? You didn't fish with a shiner. You got a little baby eel. And they sold those just like hotcakes. We've lost that economic impact. And the food for the fish. The migratory schools aren't here for the birds to swoop in and get."

The sun was high and hot. Bob and I are used to pushing off at sunrise. Erika said, "The dam is getting rid of itself, basically. It's deteriorating. "

"The Army Corps of Engineers is not fixing it as it deteriorates?"

"We're hoping not," Erika said. "I don't want them to fuss and argue about minimum flow levels, I don't want them to fuss and argue about nutrient levels. The St. Johns River Water Management District did a wonderful study, and it shows we can mitigate any negative impact; a natural flowing sand-bottom river cleans itself up and helps get rid of the phosphates." She shook her head. "We're denying the St. Johns River of a spring run. Marion County has lost the springs. We have dead trees sticking out of the water and a dam."

I could tell that Erika was a believer in environmental causes and had a lot to say. Bob and I listened, occasionally probing with a question or two. I wanted to learn, and so did Bob.

She turned away. "All right. Let's get started."

We put on our life preservers. "This is a remote area," Captain Erika said. "We will not have phone service to call for a taxi or ambulance."

"Rats. I have the Uber app," Bob said.

Straight-faced, Erika said, "What's an Uber?"

For once, Bob was stumped, then he began stammering, "Well, it's a—"

"Kidding," Erika said, as she handed him a life vest. "We aren't in the city anymore."

Gotcha, I thought. We all laughed, briefly.

Captain Erika turned to safety instructions. "In the center are a list of things that can go awry." She read aloud a placard containing a list of disasters, including bomb threats and oil spills. Safety precautions on commercial or rented crafts always seem to center on unlikely scenarios. Once, before going out on Crystal River, Bob and I watched a video in which the narrator solemnly instructed us to not stab the manatees.

The only disaster I've ever experienced in a boat is going aground. I wanted to ask Captain Erika if that was a concern. Would we have to get out and haul the boat like Katherine Hepburn and Humphrey Bogart in *The African Queen*? Then I remembered that the water was "high."

Bob asked, "Need some help with the lines?"

Captain Erika shook her head and deftly undid the lines and backed us out of the channel. The pier receded. She called out to a passing pontoon boat, "Didja all do any good?" The boaters say something unintelligible. Erika said, "If I didn't have any overhead, I'd do better than you."

We glided on satiny waters banked by hyacinths. The water reflected on the canvas hood, pulsing like waves. Butterflies hovered over the floating green islands.

The Florida Defenders of the Environment say on their website: "The ability to 'read' a landscape provides the kind of pleasure that comes from a knowledge of Bach or Shakespeare or Van Gogh. It is a pleasure that increases with your knowledge and understanding of the ecology of Florida, and it lasts an entire lifetime."

This description paints the river dweller as an artist, a human of a rare and refined sensibility.

Richard, who had been quiet until now, said, "Wouldn't you just love to have an inland waterway that connects to the ocean? I mean, as a boater, I think that would be fantastic."

Captain Erika, being the environmentalist that she is, chose to ignore Richard's observation and speak more to what's in her heart. She said, "Some people try to say that without the dams, the river would dry up. But the river could accommodate steamboats without dams."

She stood in the starboard helm, steering and keeping up a running stream of commentary. "When I was a kid, we couldn't wait to get out on the river, and we had a crystal-clear spring creek running right in front of the house. It was a log landing and it came across Browning Creek, named after the Browning family. And then, of course, the Eureka cut came in and went across our property. The barge canal came through and came right to our front door and stopped. I watched what was the perfect front yard fall into a mudhole. Totally inundated with hyacinths. Then, they'd come through with herbicides."

She pointed toward the stern and beyond. "That's the barge canal behind us. Going north. The impact here is they can raise the heights, back it up two or three feet." She pointed toward some flooded trees. "This was downtown Eureka; there used to be commercial wharfs here. This is our first highway into the center part of the state."

We passed the round concrete monolith stationed in the river, which we remembered from our last kayak trip. Erika gestured ahead. "This raised the iron grated bridge. They've replaced it with a viewing platform."

"That was a street right there," Bob said.

"Yes, that was the original Highway 16." We passed the landing to the Ocklawaha Canoe Outpost. Trees leaned out into the water. We approached a bridge.

Bob said, "This is a newer bridge. This was for the barge canal."

It is an immense, monstrous structure. As we got closer, we heard cars passing overhead.

Captain Erika directed our attention back to the river. "The water has a lot of tannin in it." I looked down into its tea-colored depths. "Sitting up high, it gathers tannic acid from the tree roots."

Bob said, "I remember coming out from the Silver River where it joined with the Ocklawaha. Toward the upper river, the water was just standing still."

Erika said, "That is controlled by a lock downside of Lake Griffin. Moss Bluff. If they drop the water weight levels too much, people complain. Moss Bluff can change overnight, two or three feet of water."

We passed logs that looked like gators. She pointed. "Cardinal flowers off to the right." Tall spikes with vivid red flowers flaunted their colors in a shady spot.

"I never saw those before," Richard said.

"We have a lot of native plants through here," Erika said. "We're coming off the Eureka cut. We're about nine miles north of Gores Landing."

The river was full of the reflections of rippled clouds. Beams of sunlight, bright as lasers, shone through the trees. Captain Erika said, "They used to log up and down this waterway."

Cruising with Captain Erika in Eureka.

"The last time we went through here, the water was crystal clear," Bob said.

"You could see the bottom," I said.

Richard said, "You come out here when it's cooler, you can actually see the leaves change color like up north. It's nice."

"Do you know where the old steamboat landings were?" I asked.

Captain Erika said, "Well, Eureka was one."

I have an old map of the tourist route of the Hart line steamboats and landings with colorful names, such as "Needles Eye," "Rough and Ready Cut" and "Hell's Half Acre." I assume Hart came up with those names based on his experience as a stagecoach driver. In fact, his entire life was based on transportation vehicles, as was his death; he fell from a trolley car in Atlanta when he was attending a business meeting there in 1895.

"How far is it from where we started in the other direction?" I asked. "To where it meets the St. Johns?"

"About twenty-six miles," Captain Erika said.

"A day's paddle?"

"No," Bob said, emphatically.

I raised my eyebrows at my loving husband of twenty-plus years. Perhaps he was learning that not all endeavors are doable in one day. As if reading my mind, Captain Erika added, "You'd better be athletic."

The perfect exclamation point, I thought, then inquired if there was anywhere to camp ahead.

"It depends," Captain Erika said. "The water could be too high." She steered for a while before picking up the conversation. "Today, the water has a pretty good current—this is good. Some of the biggest trees are right back here. That's Laurel oak. Live oak. Pine."

Except for what was cut in preparation for Rodman Reservoir and Eureka Reservoir as part of the Cross-Florida Barge Canal project in the late 1960s, the trees that are left haven't changed much. According to Paul Nosca, the "Ocklawahaman," who maintains a "Free the Ocklawaha" Facebook page, the last time the Ocklawaha cypress and the floodplain swamps were extensively timbered was before 1940. Nowadays, some trees marked as a "fire hazard" around the uplands of Rodman Reservoir are timbered at least once a year. That amount may grow for surprisingly ecological reasons. The federal government promotes research into building with wood, hoping to revive the domestic timber industry and reduce the manufacturing of carbon and steel, which accounts for 10 percent of greenhouse-gas emissions. But wood carries its own problems. I think of some of the creatures that feed on branches and twigs.

I asked, "Why is that I hear no cicadas?"

Richard perked up and said, "That's for when it's late spring or summer."

Captain Erika nodded her head in approval; apparently, she felt no need to add a comment to Richard's observation on winged insects and turned to another topic. "This is a summer town. I saw a little jaguarondi the other night. I was excited about that."

Bob asked, "What is that?"

"It's a little cat. Looks like a weasel. The adults are about twice the size of a housecat, grayish black in color, with a long tail. Its ears are the same color front to back. They're from Central America. They live in the scrub. Feral. Very secretive. Hard to spot."

"They only come out at night, I think," Richard said. "That's when I used to see them."

Captain Erika said, "It's a wild territory."

A gator glided parallel to the tree roots, his rough hide almost camouflaged by the water. Bob got up to take a picture. Usually, when he stood in a boat or a canoe or a kayak, it was to take a picture. He'd forgotten his fishing pole.

Captain Erika said, "One of the main things to come here to see is a huge dugout canoe." On an inside bend, submerged in the tea-colored water, we could see it. "Not a recent canoe, but a Timucuan canoe. Ten thousand years old."

It looked like a log under the water, protruding out of the bank, partially covered in sand and tree limbs. When we studied it more closely, we could see the distinct outline of the hand-hewn vessel. Pretty neat, I thought.

We rounded another bend. Captain Erika motioned ahead and said, "This is Richard's and my front yard, so to speak. This is our community pontoon boat dock here. We've got a little walkway back up into high ground. The barge canal goes off through the woods. On the map I showed you, it's a little green track. If you look back here, you see the locks in the earth and dam. That's the gates. Way back past the locks is the bridge. The treetops kind of cover it up. The pilings were to wait your turn for the barge to push you through the locks. Two locks to get you up, two locks to get you down. They said, 'It's just two locks.' And we're like, 'What're we, going over Niagara to get out?'"

The water level would be different from one level to another. Still, Erika's point was that the boat would only be going up a few feet. Why all the locks?

Bob said, "It didn't seem wide enough."

Captain Erika said: "Exactly. This was a project thought up in the 1800s with wooden ships. And the canal was to have been dug much deeper than the twelve feet that it ended up with. By the time the Cross-Florida Barge Canal was funded, we had iron, we had diesel engines, we had motors."

I'm reminded that over one hundred years ago, the Army Corps of Engineers had their eyes on the Ocklawaha "as a cost-effective waterway across the state." The aim was to drastically reduce the mileage between shipping routes from the Gulf of Mexico to the Atlantic Ocean and avoid having to circumnavigate around the tip of Florida's long peninsula. Maps of the proposed canal show that it would have effectively cut the northern part of the state in half. It was an economic move at a time when there were few accessible paths through the Florida scrubland, let alone paved roads. And, like the old watchtowers and forts in the south, it would eradicate foreign threats to U.S. warships. All of this occurred during the "conservationist" environmental era, when nature would be protected only if there was not a pressing engineering project at hand. Nature was something that worked for people—not the other way around.

We motored past pilings that stood like mute tributes to the ambitions of dead men. Captain Erika said, "This is still Eureka Cut. The river is older than the St. Johns."

Richard said, "This is where I've seen monkeys. I didn't know they came this far. I knew they had them in Silver Springs."

Captain Erika said, "They're vegetarians. They'll eat spiders, they'll eat frogs. They stay along the riverbanks."

Still, there are tales of aggressive behavior among the primates. All boaters should keep them at more than arm's length.

We motored on. Captain Erika said, "This is the spillway channel that runs out the spillway gates at Eureka dam. All the fish are stopped right there. They have to go up dead stagnant water, canal water; it's not the river that they're following."

The spillway is used to control the release of flows from the dam into a downstream riverbed. The water looked dark, tannic, devoid of flow.

As mentioned earlier in this chapter, elevated water levels weigh down on the lost springs in the Ocklawaha and keep them from flowing. This was documented in a 2007 special publication put out by the St. Johns River Water Management District about the submerged springs. Stagnant water is the cause of fish kills and algae bloom. All along the east side of the river, small springs emerge, bubbling in areas that don't have as much water flooding over them, so they still have an ability to flow. They could be teacup size or as small as your little finger.

We were silent for a moment. Erika said, "On my left, there's string lilies."

String lilies, also known as "swamp lilies," grow in the wetlands along riverbanks and swamps. They bloom in the summer with irregular white flowers and an enticing odor. Richard says, "Those white ones? I don't think I've ever seen them before."

Erika pointed out native plants as we traveled downstream. "Pickerelweed, spatterdock, dark green elephant plants, which are species of taro actually brought here for food. Whatever's in front of that is native plants. They're good plants that take up the phosphates and nitrogen."

Pickerelweed spikes with small purple flowers. Its seeds and leaves are edible. Spatterdock is a floating rooted plant bursting with yellow flowers used in medicine to stop bleeding or to reduce swelling. The roots and seeds are also edible. The green elephant "ears" grow in wetlands and are considered an invasive species along the Gulf Coast. The sun was hot

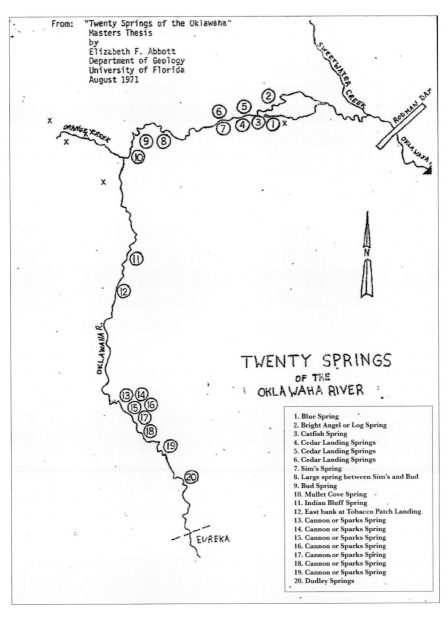

From: "Twenty Springs of the Oklawaha"
Masters Thesis
by
Elizabeth F. Abbott
Department of Geology
University of Florida
August 1971

TWENTY SPRINGS
OF THE
OKLAWAHA RIVER

1. Blue Spring
2. Bright Angel or Log Spring
3. Catfish Spring
4. Cedar Landing Springs
5. Cedar Landing Springs
6. Cedar Landing Springs
7. Sim's Spring
8. Large spring between Sim's and Bud
9. Bud Spring
10. Mullet Cove Spring
11. Indian Bluff Spring
12. East bank at Tobacco Patch Landing
13. Cannon or Sparks Spring
14. Cannon or Sparks Spring
15. Cannon or Sparks Spring
16. Cannon or Sparks Spring
17. Cannon or Sparks Spring
18. Cannon or Sparks Spring
19. Cannon or Sparks Spring
20. Dudley Springs

Ocklawaha "Lost Springs" map.

despite the canopy. The river was like a mirror to the sky. Clouds floated in the water. The boat hummed down the river and then came back. At some point, we dozed off. The tour was about two hours.

Later, on the way home, Bob and I got so lost without GPS service that we ended up in Palatka and took four hours to get home. However, we made the best of it and stopped in at Niko's Pizza, an Italian restaurant at the intersection of Highway 19 and State Road 20. We figured that with the parking lot filled with cars and trucks, it had to be good, and we were not disappointed. The meat ravioli was delicious.

We vowed—not for the first time—to bring a compass next time we head out on the river.

6

LOST SPRINGS

September 24, 2017

Every four years, the gates of the dam are opened for a few months,
and the Ocklawaha is allowed to run free.
—MOCA placard describing the showing of Margaret Ross Tolbert's art

There are twenty confirmed "lost" springs in the Ocklawaha River, most of them between Eureka and Rodman dam. Their locations were documented in 1971 by a University of Florida doctoral student in geology, Elizabeth Abbott, as part of a study for the Florida Defenders of the Environment (FDE). People call them "lost" because the springs are weighed down by tons of dammed-up murky water and decaying vegetation. These were groundwater springs, not too big, and some are still visible during drawdowns of the Rodman dam. During the last drawdown, in 2015, an artist, a filmmaker, a riverkeeper, an environmental historian, river guides and naturalists set out to immortalize the event.

The result was an art exhibition at MOCA (Museum of Contemporary Art) on Laurel Street in Jacksonville, across from Hemming Park. The park, which faces the museum, is a place still lorded over by a Confederate soldier on a pedestal whose base is fringed by the homeless. On a warm fall Sunday, there seemed to be a lull to the afternoon, the sunlight falling in thick slabs on the beige and brick municipal buildings of downtown. On a street corner, a man's arm arced lazily through the air holding a gigantic hoop from which drifted shiny soap bubbles.

The art gallery was cold as Bob and I climbed three flights of stairs to see the exhibit. Large canvases of abstract oils titled with the names of springs—Cannon, Catfish, Tobacco Patch—hung on white walls. Other titles were esoteric: Lost Springs, Sacred Springs. The showing was by Margaret Ross Tolbert, a Gainesville painter, who illuminated her artistic inspiration and her process in a film made by Matt Keene, a filmmaker and an accomplished kayaker and hiker.

Keene has paddled the entire Ocklawaha River, and this event, like water flowing downstream, brought everyone together at this place for a showing of Tolbert's art and his film, both titled *Lost Springs*. In the credits of the film, and also in the audience, was Lisa Rinaman, the St. Johns Riverkeeper; along with Mark Long, the underwater photographer; members of FDE; Captain Karen Chadwick; Captain Erika Ritter; and Paul Nosca, an independent advocate for the river known as Ocklawahaman.

The film was shown in a small auditorium a level below the first floor. Jim Draper, one of the producers of the film, took the stage along with Tolbert, Keene and Captain Chadwick. He said, "I think it's really interesting to see the way that art can be used from an activist's role."

He introduced Keene, a thirtyish, lean, red-haired man who graduated with a degree in communications from Flagler College and works for St. Johns County public schools. He described Tolbert's art as "capturing the essence of this issue":

> *One of the most poetic descriptions of the Ocklawaha is that it's a braided river where all these small little channels meander in and out through paths coming together. The story we put together reflects that. All the different channels you follow have something different to reveal. A lot of beauty and a lot of tragedy…all these different threads. But I think one of the most important threads is water and the cycle of water through this system from the floodplain forest straying out down the Ocklawaha and to the St. Johns from the water coming out through the springs. Unfortunately, that thread did not adapt to the dam. Every three or four years, the water comes out, and we see the springs come up, and we get to retrace this braided path and see the river for what it is.*

Keene introduced Tolbert, a tall, tan and fit brunette in her early sixties. She said, "I think we're all inexorably drawn to this project, to this sad and beautiful landscape. These places, these springs, these beautiful spots, they're always kind of calling to us. So we need to go out and continue our conversation with these places, with restoring the Ocklawaha, which is so much a part of us, and which is exiled from us at this point."

The film began. There was the sound of a piano soubrette. Tolbert quoted Coleridge's "Kubla Khan" and William Bartram, the famed traveler who visited this part of Florida and the Ocklawaha River in the eighteenth century. She said, "This really was the last frontier of northeast Florida, a wilderness untainted by development."

There was the sound of birds and the vision of a beautiful river landscape composed of many colors. A voice said: "This journey to the lost springs shows us what the river could be and what it was."

The springs are named on a map. They have interesting names: Blue Spring, Bright Angel, Catfish Spring, Cedar Landing Spring, Sim's Spring, Cannon Springs (there is a cluster of these), Bud Spring, Mullet Cove Spring, Indian Bluff Spring, Tobacco Patch landing and Dudley Spring. Almost all the springs have been damaged or destroyed, and they either are not flowing at all or at minimum capacity. Some are beyond saving, such as Blue Spring, once deemed the most beautiful recreation area in Florida. But some could be restored.

As Captain Erika said, they can be of teacup size or as small as a fingertip. During the drawdown, they get going again, and all the toxic materials are flushed out. Captain Erika, who grew up on the river and piloted the pontoon boat that took the crew to the lost springs, has watched what she terms "environmental genocide":

> *Every weekend, my mother took me and my sisters out to the woods, and she'd be pointing out trees: "Look at this and remember this." The Ocklawaha has had many insults by people. When they put the Rodman dam in, it was like putting something across the throat of the river where it can't breathe.*

On the screen, images of faded newspaper clippings urging tourists to make a life in Florida are juxtaposed with photos of Tolbert swimming in the river and painting by the side of the river. "Sturgeon, deer, bear, alligator and bass. This was their Eden. This was the passageway for creation." Lisa Rinaman, the riverkeeper, appears on the screen and says:

> *The springs…should be bubbling and available for all. Soon, they'll be inundated with too much water, again, just to maintain an artificial ecosystem. And when you look at this ecosystem, you have to look at the St.*

Johns, the Ocklawaha and the Silver River all together. You free the springs, the waters of the Ocklawaha improve and you have fifteen thousand acres of floodplain that will come back to its natural state.

The film expounds on the hopeful note that some people believe it's inevitable that the springs will be freed and the Rodman dam will go away. If that happens, they say that in fewer than fifty years, the lost springs will be restored to the river. Our friend Jack Bass says it will happen a lot sooner: "Within thirty minutes, the grass will be growing and the water a-flowing."

For now, when the drawdown is over, the stagnant water comes back. The springs are lost again, drowned, until another four years pass and another drawdown exposes the raw bottom to unfiltered sunlight. The next drawdown should be in 2019 or 2020, provided Rodman dam is still standing.

"Free the Ocklawaha," Paul Nosca cried when the lights came back on. Nosca generates petitions, maintains a website and posts reams of data about the river's ecological, technical and political well-being.

Everyone in the theater pined for a free-flowing Ocklawaha and for it to happen in this decade, in this lifetime. A look at the big environmental picture confirmed it was a valid idea. Considering the stagnation imposed by the Rodman dam, the noxious bubbling foam near the spill gates, the algae blooms, the periodic fish kills—without removing the dam, how else could a person know for sure whether the river will endure?

Above: Davenport Landing.

Left: Apple snail eggs.

Above: Belted kingfisher on the Ocklawaha River.

Left: Eel grass and fish at Silver Springs.

Cardinal plant downstream on the Ocklawaha River.

Lurking gator.

Right: Our red tandem
kayak we used to travel
from Gores Landing to
the Ocklawaha Outpost.

Below: Great blue heron
in foliage by Ray's.

Left: Great white egret.

Below: Cannon Springs Fish, 2017, oil on canvas, by Margaret Ross Tolbert at the Museum of Contemporary Art in Jacksonville.

MARGARET ROSS TOLBERT
(American, born 1954)
Cannon Springs Fish, 2017
Oil on canvas
Collection of the artist.

Right: Juniper Inlet.

Below: Limpkins and pickerelweed.

Right: Little blue heron.

Below: Mouth of the
Ocklawaha River.

Anhinga in a tree on the Ocklawaha River.

Kayaks at Orange Springs.

Left: Supermoon at Orange Springs.

Below: Crossing Rodman Reservoir.

Another little blue heron.

Green heron on the Ocklawaha River.

Left: Entrance to Cannon Springs.

Below: Silver Springs State Park in the evening.

Left: Statue of Chief Osceola stabbing the Seminole treaty.

Right: Pickerelweed.

Red-bellied cooters.

Snowy egret on the Ocklawaha River.

Tiny turtle on Silver River.

Silver River turtle.

Silver Springs deer near the Silver River museum.

Left: Silver Springs Landing.

Right: St. Johns River.

Swamp lilies and a caterpillar.

Upturned tree roots on the Ocklawaha after Hurricane Irma.

Wild turkey on the Rodman Dam Loop.

7

RODMAN DAM TO THE MOUTH OF THE ST. JOHNS RIVER

October 8, 2017

The Ocklawaha River, colloquially known as the Creek, meanders through a vast hardwood swamp carpeted with poison ivy, teeming with water moccasins, and thick with alligators.
—*Bob H. Lee,* Backcountry Lawman

When Bob H. Lee, a writer whom my husband, Bob, and I met at the Florida Heritage Book Festival in St. Augustine, offered to take me and Bob out on his motorboat from the Highway 19 boat launch to the Rodman dam and then to the mouth of the Ocklawaha near the St. Johns in Palatka, I could not even pretend that we would hesitate for a minute. It was the last big segment of the river that we hadn't touched. On land, it would have been the difference between riding a bicycle up and down hills or riding a motorcycle. We opted for the motorboat. We could always go back later and explore the tributaries, cast a line and sit under the trees waiting for a bite and for the wildlife to emerge. After all, so far, Bob hadn't come close to catching even one fish.

We agreed to meet the retired game warden at the boat ramp off Highway 19. Bob (my husband) kept assuring me that he knew how to find it. Even though Bob is a notoriously good navigator, I was nervous about the location.

When we conferred with Jack Bass, he said, "Oh, yeah," as though the launch were common knowledge. My husband even showed me where it was on a map.

I woke up at 2:00 a.m. on Sunday, and we were on the road by 6:00 a.m. I stared out the window as we drove. I've heard locals say that fishing is down on the Ocklawaha River because the dam blocks a migratory path and that bait shops have actually closed in Putnam County despite annual bass fishing tournaments. In fact, some residents said that in April 2017, one-third of the anglers caught bass from the locks and the river and not from the reservoir. Proponents of Rodman dam insist that the reservoir is one of the top bass fishing locales in the nation, and they are damned proud of it. The two groups find it difficult to locate common ground on this issue, which pits avid anglers against environmental activists. I was curious to get Bob H. Lee's take on the Rodman dam.

Not wanting to miss the launch, I tried to veto Bob's stop at the Square Meal Restaurant in Salt Springs, but he insisted he could find the ramp with time to spare. Locals congregated outside, smoking, and spoke to us as we passed: "You guys lost or somethin'?"

Inside, there were square and rectangular tables. The threshold had an engraved wooden banner over the entrance in which the words "Cherish yesterday, dream tomorrow, live today" are etched. We noticed that at this hour of the morning on a weekend, the patrons heavily favored camouflage garb. Our waitress was young with plaited hair. She said, "How do? What can I get you guys to drink?"

We ordered strong coffee, and after a fine breakfast of eggs and grits, we hit the road. A half-hour later, Bob found the launch location. The boat ramp was fine. Up ahead, though, a big tree blocked the river. This was a result of Hurricane Irma. Debris was everywhere.

This was almost as bad as missing the ride. We made it, but how could we go? We had to drive to the top of the bridge to get enough phone service so I could text Bob H. Lee that the river was blocked. I supposed that was that.

So, I was surprised to see him striding toward us as at the launch, wearing wraparound shades and a camouflage baseball cap over clipped gray hair.

I said, "Hi, Bob Lee."

My husband said, "What? Are we swimming?"

It turned out that the lawman had left his boat moored under the north side of the bridge, climbed up the side and walked over the top and down to the ramp to tell us to meet him at the Davenport Landing. We demurred, instead following him north and over the crest of the Highway 19 overpass, carrying a small cooler with chicken salad sandwiches and cookies. Bob H. Lee—whom I'll hereafter refer to as Lee so as to avoid confusing between him and my husband, Bob—is a lean, tallish guy in his mid-sixties who

Backcountry lawman Bob H. Lee and Liz Randall.

seems to epitomize the meme "sixty is the new forty." Bob and I huffed to keep up with him. There was all kinds of debris on the bridge; we stepped over a dismembered deer leg.

Lee told us to avoid the poison ivy growing out of the bridge embankment. Then, we hopped on to his powerboat, an eighteen-foot flats boat made by Scout. He motored under the bridge, toward Rodman dam, and began a running commentary, taking sips from a water bottle from time to time.

Lee grew up "on the shores of a small lake in the community of Lutz, thirteen miles north of Tampa." He graduated from the University of South Florida with a degree in criminal justice. He and his wife, Karen, moved to Palatka in 1977. For years, he worked as a game and fish officer in Putnam County, staking out and nabbing poachers. In his retirement, he is a successful author of two books: *Backcountry Lawman* and *Bullets, Bad Guys, and Boat Chases*.

Lee is a gregarious man, and one accustomed to public speaking; it seemed providential to me and Bob that we had happened to run into someone who spent thirty years of his career patrolling up and down the river about which we were writing. Our omen of good luck was

A monarch butterfly on Liz's ballcap.

accentuated when a monarch butterfly perched on my baseball cap for the first few minutes of the boat ride. Lee admitted he'd never seen one so far downstream at that time of the year.

We were heading west from the Highway 19 bridge spanning a section of the old Ocklawaha River—a narrow, twisting creek with lots of wetland birds; anhingas held their wings aloft. The water was high.

Lee said, "We'll try exploring a side creek or two." He pointed aft. "I have some downstream I want to try. In a little while, if you want, we can go back upstream and put it on a plane and cruise up to Rodman dam and check out Davenport, too."

We cruised at a low speed. Bob stood at the head of the boat casting lines. Lee said, "These side creeks are sometimes impassable because of bank-to-bank logjams. The locals will go in with chainsaws and clear them out so they can fish. The Corps of Engineers usually keeps the main channel open, but they won't clear out all the side creeks. The other thing here in the springtime? You have to be careful of brushing up against a wax myrtle tree, cause they have those wasp nests in them. Boy, they can work on you if you hit them."

I said, "There's a lot of trees down." Lee was expertly maneuvering around them. I figured a man used to chasing poachers down this river in the dead of night knew what he was doing.

I relayed Jack Bass's story about the logjams to Lee. "Okay," he said, "Here's a good example coming up ahead of us." He pointed to a fallen tree, the branches barely sticking up above the surface. I didn't have a clue which way we should go.

Lee continued:

> *If you study these types of half-sunken trees long enough, you can figure out where the best path is to cross or go around without ripping the transom off the boat. What I see here is a very faint—not even a ripple, hardly—but a faint swirl all along the tree's trunk, which is hidden out of sight but just beneath the water. That tells me the trunk is not deep enough for me to motor over it, nor can I make my way over or through the canopy. We have to go around the tip of the canopy, the very end of the tree. If you look closely, you can see where other boats have cut a path through the lily pads.*

With that, our skipper skillfully made a detour through the shallows and back out into the main channel. Bob pointed to another fallen tree, and Lee said:

> *That's what we call a deadhead log right there. Not to be confused with the deadhead logs that have been timbered long ago, which is a topic we will probably touch on in a few minutes. Anyway, this log is facing downstream. What happens is the upper canopy has snapped off, and you're left with the broken top of the trunk and the root ball trapped on the bottom, and then the current pushes it over. Then you've got the broken end bobbing at the surface.*

The logjams reminded him of Roger Gunter, the famous poacher who eluded him for years and with whom he'd drawn a kind of truce since his retirement. "Now, Roger Gunter, he's also a movie star. He was on that reality TV show, *Ax Men*, for three seasons. It's on cable."

Bob said, "Oh yeah. They had guys diving off the boat into the water. "

"They had to make it dramatic," Lee said. "What I didn't know, until I interviewed him for the book, is that Gunter and his dad used to deadhead log from a barge in Rice Creek [five miles north of Palatka]. This was back in the fifties, when he was eight years old. Before they even had diving gear."

Naturally, curious, I needed to better understand, so I asked, "What does 'deadhead log' mean?"

Lee said:

> *These are logs that were cut years ago and floated out in giant rafts by timber companies. Some of them sank. They have original cut or saw marks in them. They'll be heart pine or pecky cypress, which is worth a fortune. A special permit is required from the state. You can't deadhead log without a permit, otherwise you could be charged with a felony. The show was exaggerated, but the logs they were recovering were real.*

Lee stopped to take a pull on his water bottle. Since we were riding in a motorboat, the landmarks zipped by quickly. I realized that this trip would be a blur captioned by Lee's anecdotes.

"How did you keep from hitting deadhead logs during nighttime patrols and boat chases?" I asked.

Lee chuckled and said:

> *Back then, we used a hardhat with a 110,000-candlepower aircraft landing lamp strapped to it. Lit up the creek like daylight. The trick was to continually sweep your head back and forth to pick up the subtle differences between the dark-colored snags and the lighter surface of the water. A small piece of wood sticking up could be attached to a huge log hidden just below. It was important not to hit any of them, otherwise you'd take a ride you didn't want to go on.*

I wondered what kind of training he went through to prepare for patrolling in this watery wilderness and asked him to expand on that topic. "It was all on-the-job training." Lee said. "When I began my career in 1977, I was assigned the fastest patrol boat in the state—a souped-up eighteen-foot Old Timer with a two hundred–HP Johnson bolted to the transom. My first day, I didn't know how to use the manual choke, didn't know squat."

Bob and I were sympathetic. Although we didn't own a boat then, we had been out many times with friends and witnessed many boat launches. In our experience, most motors need a lot of coaxing.

Lee elaborated:

> *The first time I took it out on patrol, I took it up here. It's a very difficult boat to drive. There's no chines on it; it'll slide out from underneath you just like that. I didn't know how to bring it alongside another vessel—first thing I did, I came up underneath the Ocklawaha 19 bridge and practiced parking next to the wooden fenders. I'm very fortunate I didn't kill myself. In fact, I barely had a full year on when my patrol boat sunk at about midnight, in this creek, when the branch from a sunken tree pulled the lever-styled drain plug out. I ended up astraddle a six-gallon gas can floating out through a gauntlet of alligators. That was a gut-check moment for me. From then on, I always made sure to put the drain plug in from the inside.*

Bob said, "We kayaked Silver River. And I was kind of surprised—at the mouth of the Ocklawaha, it seems like all the flow was in Silver River, and everything upstream seemed stagnant."

Lee said, "Since 1960, water flow has diminished by 40 percent. The less flow, the less water forcing debris out to keep a deeper channel. Back in the paddlewheel days, they had the same problems we're facing today, and that's all these trees."

I recalled reading about a lawsuit brought by the Putnam County Environmental Council against the St. Johns River Water Management District in 2015, which said pretty much the same thing about the decline in aggregate surface outflow from the Ocklawaha Chain of Lakes.

We'd motored a few miles upstream from the Highway 19 bridge when Lee pointed to a side creek off to our right and said, "This is called Dead River."

The monarch butterfly was long gone. I shivered. According to Lee, there were sometimes unsavory activities going on on Dead River, primarily poaching.

He said:

> *Back in the day, there used to be a lot of electric fishing that went on up in here. Roger Gunter, when I was interviewing him, he told me of a secret*

Dead tree debris.

Dead River.

fishing hole he had in this creek. When he put the electrodes down and turned on the machine, there were so many fish that came up, it actually lifted the boat eight inches up outta the water. He'd bulkhead the boat with six to eight hundred pounds of catfish every time. He said he never had that happen before except that one hole.

Bob said, "It doesn't kill the fish?"

Lee said, "Stuns 'em. You go up here about three quarters of a mile, and it separates into three or four different fingers. Into what they call the jungle. It's only about two to three feet deep. If you know where you're going, you can navigate through the jungle, and then you come back out on the Ocklawaha just downstream from Rodman dam. Which is where I'm going to show you next. We may end up hitting a treetop along the way."

In the open water, a gator floated, looking like a log with eyes—only slower. Lee pointed and said, "Now, there's a gator there, he's a pretty good gator. He's about a ten-footer. Seen very few gators here lately. They're all back in the swamps feeding on coons and possums because of the high water."

A quarter-mile upstream from the mouth of Dead River, Lee swept his hand to the left. "Now, this'll be Davenport Landing here. Normally, you can see a white sand beach, but because of the flood waters, it's covered up."

He slowed down and whipped his finger back downstream to a narrow creek.

That's little Johnson Creek. It goes along the hill. You got the hill and you got the water. Not much in between except for a tussock, which is a hump of decaying vegetation. The Ocala forest is one big massive hill of sugar sand which slopes down and stops right at the edge of the creek. There used to be several primitive campsites, but now the Florida Forest Service won't allow people to go in and camp there anymore. But this creek happens to come right back out underneath the culvert where the boat ramp is on Highway 19.

Bob said, "We've been here."

The Davenport Landing Historic Site is located on the northern edge of the Ocala National Forest and the southern side of the Ocklawaha River, where it flows east until its eventual confluence with the St. Johns River. The site is accessible from Forest Road 77, though there is no direct vehicular access to the site; I remembered driving down a dirt road for a long time in the Ocala National Forest, passing a campground and standing on a bluff looking out on the beach and the river for the first time. I was here with Bob last year, catching our first glimpse of the Ocklawaha. Some things looked different from the water; some looked the same.

The beach we'd seen from the bluff was submerged in river water. I wondered if the gator we just saw was the same one who had cruised by at 11:00 a.m. last year, and for how many years, or decades, had it been around here? Alligators can be centenarians; they have long lives.

For the first time, I found a landmark on the river, and I felt familiar with the environment. The early afternoon sky hovered just above the trees and the lush hyacinths. I had a picture of it on my screensaver at home.

"Davenport is a historic landing," Lee said. "It's a steamboat landing—the last high bluff that steamboats passed as they made their way downriver. It's also an Indian encampment. There's a small cemetery up here, too—maybe half a dozen graves."

As we continued our journey upstream, Lee kept up a running dialogue, explaining how the bottom of the Ocklawaha is shaped. "The outside currents are deep, the inside shallow. That's because the current places more pressure on an outside curve, actually digging into the bank, causing greater erosion, which results in greater depth."

Cruisin' alligator.

That was good to know. I remembered Bob and I spinning like tops in our cheap kayaks the first time we went out.

Lee added:

In the old days, outlaw commercial fishermen would run illegal hoop nets in this creek. They'd drop them in the water and let them roll up under the side of banks over these outside curves. Typically, they'd empty them once a week. To retrieve the trap, they'd reach down into the water with a long pole with a hook attached on one end, snag the webbing and haul them up. You can't run wire fish traps or hoop nets in tributary, only in the main body of the St. Johns River. The reason why the tributaries are off limits to commercial fishing devices is because this is where the channel cats [catfish] and white cats come up to spawn. The channel catfish get up to forty pounds, white cats about seven.

I said, "What kinds of cats do you see in this river?"

Lee said:

Basically, there's four species: the yellow cat or the butter cat, the speckled or brown bullhead, then there's the white cat and the channel cat. These last two are the more preferred fish by seafood markets. They have what's called the "white meat," which is flaky and has a mild flavor. During the springtime, the white cat and the channel cat spawn in the creeks. Whereas the yellow and speckled cat spawn in the shallows of the river. In February, they go into the eel grass. People used to go in there with spears and gig them, 'cause there's so many. They're considered a nongame fish. You can legally shoot them with a bow and arrow or a gig. But always check fishing regulations, because the laws can change.

He briefly paused to drink from his water bottle. "There is a name for just about every side creek." I remembered from the *Lost Springs* film that Matt Keene called the creeks "braids."

Lee continued, "Particularly, downstream from Highway 19. I've seen them on the map. Some can be navigated by canoe, some not. Good bass fishing. Some of the creeks have names like, Bear, Johnson, Turpentine."

Clearly, Lee was revisiting his game warden days. It was interesting to know the environmental history from the point of view of a member of law enforcement. Lee was an advocate for wildlife, fish and the laws governing their protection. He told us we were about ten miles from Rodman dam.

Bob said, "Why do people poach?"

Lee said:

> *There's a variety of reasons for why they poach. Let's start with the weekend warrior. Here's the scenario: There's a couple of guys at home, they watched the late-night show, they're drinking beer. And it comes two o'clock in the morning, they're bored out of their gourd. One of them slams a beer down, looks at his buddy and says, "Let's go kill a deer." But they have a problem—neither one owns a gun. So, they go down the street to Joe's house and knock on the door. Joe says he's got a gun and is tired of his "ole lady" yelling at him, so he's more than ready to go. They hop in a truck, drive down, say, Highway 19 in the Ocala National Forest, shining a spotlight. And lo and behold, a game warden happens to be sitting in the bushes and pulls out behind them. End of story. These guys wanted a little excitement and some venison, but they got more than they bargained for. You can't shoot deer at night. Period. It gets back to the basic rules of "fair chase." It's not fair chase to go out and shoot a deer when they're mesmerized by a bright spotlight."*

Lee shook his head. "Second scenario: Then we have the guys who are kill-crazy. They gotta kill deer. Even to the point where they'll hit them with their vehicle. Some may kill eighty to a hundred deer a year. They love to draw blood, to kill, they're addicted—"

Old Florida Fish and Wildlife Conservation Commission sign spotted on the Ocklawaha River with Bob Lee.

I interrupted, "Bob, Bob, a gator." The reptile was about six feet long and sunning himself on a log near the east bank. Bob sprang to his feet, camera at the ready. Maybe it was the time of year, but we had not seen so many gators in one trip.

Lee said, "Good eye—you spotted him way back there."

Bob said, "I didn't see him." He snapped a few shots.

Lee pointed. "He came off that hump."

I apologized to Lee for the interruption and asked him to continue, which he did:

> *The final scenario is a rare occurrence anymore, and that would be the professional poacher. Someone like Roger Gunter falls into that category. He's the real deal and extremely cunning. If I were to sum him up in a single sound-bite, I would ask you to imagine a cross between a modern-day Daniel Boone and a fictional Crocodile Dundee. He thinks, he plans, he evaluates everything ahead of time. He watches you. He scans your patrol radio. Unlike a lot of poachers I've known, Roger managed to keep a really good job as a supervisor for the Georgia Pacific paper company for thirty-five years. The poaching was just icing on the cake.*

We moved off into another creek that ran south from a security cable and jugs that kept boaters from entering the dam's spillway. Lee motioned ahead and changed the subject. "This body of water we're in right now, it's still is part of the old river channel that was cut off when they made the dam. There's very little flow, but the fish in it are quite good, at times."

Bob said, "I've never even had a bite out here."

Lee said, "If you anchor out here? You can probably kill the black bass. Although, I'm saying that, but I didn't see many folks fishing at the dam when we passed it earlier."

I asked, "What's your position on the dam? Keep it or destroy it?"

Lee ruminated before saying, "Personally, I've vacillated on this over the years."

He took a deep breath:

> *When I first got here, I said blow it up. I'm a firm believer that everything should go back to its natural state. Then, when I saw how many people enjoy fishing Rodman Lake, I said, well, let it stay. Now, that I've gotten older, I've reversed my position. I say, blow it up.*

He paused before continuing:

> *I am not concerned about the tournament bass fishing. I am not concerned about the few professional guys who go on Rodman Lake. They can go somewhere else and fish. But what concerns me is: What about all these subsistence fishermen at Rodman dam? In the springtime, you'll find two hundred people there. A lot of them can hardly scrape enough dollars to afford half a tank of gas to get there.*

Lee looked directly at us. "For them,"—he gestured toward the water—"these are their groceries. If the dam is breached, will they have the same fishing opportunities they have now?"

Bob asked, "What about Moss Bluff?"

"Were people fishing there?" I asked. "I don't remember."

"They were fishing both sides," Bob said.

I asked Lee, "You're saying there's more fish in the Rodman reservoir?"

Lee reiterated:

> *What I'm saying is, if it's breached, could anyone catch the volume of fish they're catching now? And what are the positives of breaching the dam? Well, a lot. Finally, you can have real ecotourism, and maybe for Palatka, they could replicate the old steamboat trips up to Silver Springs and back. An argument is made that it's gonna take two hundred years for the swamp to reestablish. Poppycock.*

Lee readjusted his baseball cap to make his point:

> *Within twenty-five to thirty years, you're gonna have trees twenty-five to thirty feet high. I firmly believe that. It might be kind of a mess starting out until it gets deep and shady and a lot of that secondary growth is knocked back and naturally dies off. I believe it would be reestablished a lot quicker than most folks think. But many of the Putnam County politicians are adamant about saving the dam. They feel saving Rodman Lake is going to save Putnam County. I strongly disagree. There's a zillion places to fish in this area. Look at Welaka, look at the St. Johns River, big Lake George, Crescent Lake and Lakes Lochloosa and Orange over in Alachua County, right next door.*

Lee added, "But getting rid of the dam doesn't mean fishing is going to be stopped. There will still be fishing. But keep in mind—"

Bob and I leaned forward. I began recording video on my phone.

> *Striped bass, at one time, naturally reproduced in the Ocklawaha River. There's a general feeling because of Rodman dam, they do not. My understanding is their eggs need a certain amount of time suspended in rolling clear water for them to ripen. Now, about the time I came here, in '77, our biologists did some tests. They took a year off from stocking the river with striped bass. After a year, they checked for fingerling stripers—they found zero, which meant there was no natural reproduction.*

He made an "O" with his thumb and forefinger. "Because the dam stops the natural flow, apparently, it prevents the eggs from being suspended in free-flowing water for the time necessary for them to hatch."

There *was* a study in 1977 conducted by the Saint Johns River Water Management District (SJRWMD), which, among other things, provided an analysis of the "relative abundance" of several fish species since the creation of the reservoir. They concluded that some species of bass decreased in the riverine zone.

It is a fact that striped bass have not been seen in the Ocklawaha River upstream from Rodman dam since its construction—an impediment that makes it difficult for the game fish to reproduce. Largemouth bass may flourish in a dammed reservoir, but other species—such as striped bass, blue crabs, shad, eels, manatees and shortnose sturgeon—may diminish or even vanish.

Later, I talked to a fisheries administrator, Ryan Hamm, of the Florida Fish and Wildlife Conservation Commission (FWC), who said that they tried stocking Atlantic striped bass in the Ocklawaha in 2014, but the efforts failed: "We have not seen it [striped bass] anywhere," he said. "Maybe they're there in such low levels, we haven't seen them. This is the southern end of their range. They need cool water to survive; they need freshwater springs as a thermal refuge. They've been found in Silver Glen off Lake George in the summer."

There always seem to be catfish, and I asked Lee about that. Lee said, "The catfish here in the river? Particularly in the spring and early summer? It's crazy. Interestingly, there's only a handful of people commercial-fishing for them anymore. The monster fish farms in the Mississippi delta diminished the need for wild-caught catfish."

We were a mile or so upstream from the mouth of the Ocklawaha River on the right (or south) side, keeping in mind that the Ocklawaha generally runs east and west downstream from Rodman dam. "This is Hart's Swirl," Lee said. "It's the deepest hole downstream from Rodman dam, about thirty-five feet deep. During the legal alligator-hunting season, when my son was about eighteen, we harpooned a tremendous alligator here one night. But we lost him when he swam down and got wrapped around a submerged tree."

It was getting to be late in the afternoon—about time to wrap things up. Lee glanced at the sun and said, "I want to see the rest of the river." Forty minutes later, we were not far from the St. Johns River. A vista was opening up in front of me. The Ocklawaha River winds, almost doubling on itself in places. Sometimes, it seemed as narrow as a creek, hence its nickname. It turns and twists toward one side and then another, sometimes running so close to the trees that the insects on the branches jump on paddlers. You can seldom see more than a few hundred yards ahead. It is a trip through a dense growth of partly submerged cypress. Then, it reaches the St. Johns River.

People have told me that the seven-mile run of the Silver River was the most beautiful sight they'd ever seen. Certainly, the Ocklawaha River had captured our imagination, interest and even affection. But I never realized that this juncture from the mouth of the Ocklawaha to the St. Johns River was such a contrast; I felt a surge of energy almost as though my soul were widening. The sun was like a hot copper coin in the sky, and a pelican made a lazy swooping flight across the blue cloudless expanse just above a green tree line of heavily forested hammock. A fierce wind drew across a point in the wide, winding river, creating ripples and almost blowing the baseball cap off my head.

The St. Johns River is a 310-mile northward-flowing passage that was selected as one of fourteen American Heritage Rivers in 1997. Lisa Rinaman, the current St. Johns Riverkeeper, said her first sight of the St. Johns River "sealed the deal" for her when she moved from Arkansas to Florida. Rinaman's work as a riverkeeper ensures pure, plentiful and uncontaminated water for the public. This is not an easy task. In 2008, the St. Johns River was listed as the sixth–most endangered waterway in the nation. It became endangered because the St. Johns Water Management District continues to allow permits for excessive withdrawals, by pumping, of river water.

To Bob and me, it looked like the edge of the St. Johns River continued where the Ocklawaha doubled back. We were surrounded by blue water, a reflection of the open sky. A low, glitter-painted bass boat with a big outboard engine skidded up the river and took off. Lee slowed to a stop, and the wake buffeted us about a bit. Lee, Bob and I swayed slightly in our seats. For the first time, I was glad I was a novice to these waters, because it was all new to me. After all, you can only see something once for the first time. I felt sure I would never forget the complexity and simplicity of the scene: the juncture, the Ocklawaha, the largest tributary to the St. Johns River flowing onward, north, toward the Atlantic Ocean. It was hard to believe that the magnificent vista before us could one day be a putrid pool of algae blooms and Microcystis.

The mental image of the confluence of two great Florida rivers was my personal illustration for the day. No matter what happened, it would always reside in my memory.

Part II

CAMPING AND A RESEARCH FORAY

8

PADDLE FLORIDA

October 1, 2017

*We cannot live without the Earth or apart from it, and something is shriveled in
a man's heart when he turns away from it and concerns himself only with the
affairs of men.*
—*Marjorie Kinnan Rawlings*

I was sure that Bob and I would be missing the crux of our adventure if we
did not spend more time on the river, preferably camping. However, Bob
refused to camp willy-nilly at random sites along the river. The main reason
was ticks, defined as "a superfamily of bloodsucking arachnids that are
larger than the mites, and attach themselves to warm-blooded vertebrates to
feed, and impart important vectors of infectious diseases." I had to admit,
ticks were attracted to Bob like vampires. After a jaunt on the road *near* some
woods, he was apt to pick up a tick or two.

The only solution was to find someone else who knew something about
camping along the river—or, even better, someone who would know what to
do in the event the narrow river was blocked by fallen trees, which was likely
after Hurricane Irma.

I first read about Paddle Florida, Inc., during a random Internet search.
One day, I Googled "Ocklawaha, camping, kayaking," and Paddle Florida
came up. Its logo was: "Inspiring. Meaningful. Adventure." The website
featured photographs of manatees and kayakers, a range of colorful
domed tents and high-end kayaks ready for launch. One of the company's

sponsors is Visit Florida, the official state travel, tourism and vacation website for Florida, which partners with various water management agencies and other Florida paddling and trail organizations.

Paddle Florida was offering a four-day kayaking and camping trip, called the "Ocklawaha Odyssey," the first week in December. It wasn't the only trip the paddling organization was sponsoring. There was the Suwanee River Wilderness Trail; the Flagler Coastal Wildlife Immersion; the Wild, Wonderful Withlacoochee; the Great Calusa Blueway; and the Choctawhatchee Challenge.

The names may have made them sound like YMCA camps, but the trips catered to a growing cadre of mostly older Floridians who wanted a vacation as unlike a theme park as possible.

Terrified that other kayakers would fill up the accommodation list for the Ocklawaha Odyssey (since they could only take seventy-five people), I called and talked to a guy named Bill Richards, the executive director of Paddle Florida. I immediately signed up. The Ocklawaha Odyssey offered by Paddle Florida, Inc., was the solution to several kayaking problems Bob and I had encountered on our own.

A Penske truck would transport our kayaks, tents and belongings from site to site. Paddle Florida would provide all the food (and I would have gone for that reason alone). As a former home economics teacher, I was dying to see how someone would cater food for almost one hundred people at remote, primitive camping sites.

Then, there was the itinerary:

> DAY 1: *Silver Springs State Park to Ray Wayside Park 6 miles to Gores Landing 10.5 miles*
> DAY 2: *Gores Landing to Eureka Boat Ramp Ocklawaha Canoe Outpost 9.5 miles*
> DAY 3: *Ocklawaha Canoe Outpost to Payne's Landing 7.5 to Orange Springs Boat Ramp 13.2 miles*
> DAY 4: *Orange Springs Boat Ramp to Rodman Campground 6.7 Miles*

Bob and I had already paddled most of the launches on the itinerary with the exception of Orange Springs and the Rodman Reservoir. The trip was broken into four days of paddling. At the end of the trip, a shuttle would take us from the Rodman Reservoir to our starting point at Silver Springs State Park.

I broached all this with Bob in the evening.

"We could back out," I said. "But where else would we get the chance to kayak and *camp* on the river? With people who know what they're doing? I hope!"

Bob said, "This is in December? It could be cold."

"Yes!" I said. "Cold! Less in the way of ticks."

This line of thinking helped with getting Bob to agree to the trip. I told him there was nothing to worry about—that I had already rented a kayak from the Ocklawaha Canoe Outpost in Eureka; it was the same Old Town tandem kayak we'd used before, because our light-yellow kayaks would never make it over almost forty-six miles of flooded river. Mike O'Neal, or his wife, Sheri, would transport the tandem kayak to Silver Springs on the morning of the launch, December 1. Then, they would pick it up from Rodman Campground (located on the east side of Rodman Lake) on December 4, after the trip ended.

The paddling group was spending one night at the Outpost landing in Eureka, and there was an option to rent one of the little prefab cabins I was so taken with the previous spring. I made reservations for that night. The rest of the time, we would sleep in the tent.

It wasn't as expensive as, say a four-day trip to Disney World. It wasn't cheap, either. The itinerary warned that this was not a trip with a lot of luxuries, but it still cost $460 apiece, plus around $300 (combined) for the four-day kayak and one-night cabin rental.

Fortunately, we had some of the necessary supplies. Our daughter Courtney had just moved home from Pensacola, where she had spent a lot of time tubing and camping, which is what proud Argonauts of the University of West Florida did (hopefully, in addition to attending classes). Amazingly, she graduated with honors before she moved back in with us, and she agreed to loan us her tent, an Ozark Trail purchased from Walmart. Bob went into the attic and brought down a thirty-year-old down sleeping bag, rather worse for the wear but ready to have its final camping swan song before it was retired forever.

Bob and I put up Courtney's tent in the living room of our home. We pumped up the air mattress and spread the ancient sleeping bag on it. We crawled inside and lay on our backs and stared at the nylon roof. There was a flap, which Bob said we could peel back to look at the stars. Courtney's cat, Frances, walked across the top of the tent, which caved in a bit.

"This will do," I said.

Bob sighed the disgruntled sigh of a middle-aged man who liked his creature comforts and observed, "The air mattress is leaking."

It was true—we had sunk down to the floor. We would have to replace the mattress.

There are a lot of details that go into planning a camping trip. Fortunately, aside from the leaky air mattress, we found the perfect trip—orchestrated by someone else but exactly suited to our needs. All we had to do was take a couple of days off work and show up, with our gear, at Silver Springs State Park on December 1, 2017, at 5:00 p.m.

We were not the slightest bit concerned about the trip, even though we had never attempted anything like it. We were just happy the opportunity had materialized. We were happy to be on the river for four days. This kind of attitude—a faith in luck and a lack of foresight—had fueled all of our adventures on the river so far. Why should this trip be any different?

9

SILVER SPRINGS STATE PARK

December 1, 2017

Both intelligence and, for those of you who wish, the Bible, dictate that man is to have dominion over all the resources of the Earth.
—*Thomas Burton Adams Jr., secretary of state of Florida from 1961 to 1971*

It was almost a full moon, and Bob removed the tent's cover flap. We stared through mesh into the sky. By December 3, the lunar cycle would evolve into a "supermoon," an event when the full moon is at the closest point of its orbit to the Earth. It makes the moon look extra close and bright — up to 14 percent bigger and 30 percent brighter than a full moon at its farthest point from Earth. Already, the moon looked extra close and bright. We found Orion's belt and talked as the supermoon breasted the clouds inch upon inch.

Earlier, we had arrived at Silver Springs State Park at around 4:00 p.m. Registration was set up on the south side, and Bob and I met Bill Richards, Paddle Florida's executive director, and Janice Hindman, Paddle Florida's volunteer coordinator and board chair for the Florida Society for Ethical Ecotourism. We had to sign some papers releasing the organization from any liability in case Bob and I had some kind of a kayak mishap, which they explained to us in detail.

Paddlers can become trapped underwater in their kayaks by a phenomenon called the "tree strainer." The tree strainer can occur when a kayaker is coming around a blind bend in a flowing stream and attempts to skirt a fallen tree. Erosion of the riverbank is usually the cause of the fallen tree (also called "widow-makers"), and in our case, Hurricane Irma was sure to have downed a lot of them. If a kayaker gets stuck in a strainer, the water pressure can suck the paddler under the tree and trap him there.

This was an event Bob and I had never considered in our initial forays onto the river. In fact, I would recommend that paddlers wishing to emulate a journey like ours hit the river with an experienced guide the first time, as we did with Jack Bass. But our second trip, paddling upstream in flimsy kayaks, could have been a disaster. I realized that we had been lucky.

After we signed all the papers releasing Paddle Florida from any responsibility if we fecklessly succumbed to a tree strainer or any other calamity, Bill and Janice gave us a tote bag containing a map, coupons, a T-shirt and a whistle, which we were to blow if we got lost or stuck on a tree branch. Dinner was at six in the Silver Springs State Park cafeteria. Then, they directed us through a gate to the southern end of the camp, which was identified with a sign: "Primitive Campground."

I had spent most of my camping career in places like Disney's Fort Wilderness and St. Augustine's Anastasia State Park. Primitive camping did not include running water, although there was a bathroom facility, one of those plastic sheds with a vacuum toilet like an airplane's—a slight step up from a porta-potty. A wire mesh fence separated us from the sounds of traffic. All around us, people were erecting their tents on the dry winter grass.

We walked around to look at the sleeping accommodations. Most of the nylon and polyester tents were domed like ours, but one was a "backpack tent" that weighed one and a half pounds and slept one (obviously). There was a free-standing hammock tent, too.

Bob put up our tent in five minutes, and I inflated the air mattress and spread our ancient sleeping bag over it. Then, we were free to walk around Silver Springs State Park until dinner and the pre-paddle briefing. The park closed at 5:00 p.m. every day, so we would have the place to ourselves.

Bob and I had been to Silver Springs State Park a few times already, so we knew its history. We knew that it is the gateway to the Ocala National Forest. The springs feed into the Silver River, a five-mile stream that flows east from the springs to the Ocklawaha River. It was a shooting location for some of the Tarzan movies and the home of the glass-bottom boat ride—the brainchild of Hubbard Hart, among others. It was also the subject of controversy in recent years as the flow of the river dropped and algae blooms started making an appearance because of nitrate runoff related to development in Marion County.

Still, to our eyes, it was a place of wondrous beauty. Near the tree-lined entrance was an ornate lamppost, a gift shop and three flagpoles. To the left were shops and restaurants. To the right was a waiting area and loading dock for glass-bottom boat tours. Staring straight down into the springs, we could see fish moving amid the eel grass.

We tried to find the *I Spy* statues we saw when we had been in the area last year with Jack Bass. Clean and pristine in 2016, the white statues were now green with algae and almost indiscernible sixty feet below in the spring waters.

Passing shaded pavilions with benches and white rocking chairs, we walked toward the Twin Oaks Mansion area. We passed the statue of Chief Osceola stabbing the treaty that led to the second Seminole War. There were trees with autumn leaves, even though it was December. Flocks of white ibises roosted in the trees along the water's edge on the other side of the springs. We passed the contorted loop of the old horseshoe palm tree where couples stand and take selfies to bring good luck. We passed pink trumpet flowers hanging from tangled branches, and we crossed a bridge.

Silver Springs ibis.

The mansion appeared on our left, white-pillared and surrounded by mossy trees. The park kept giraffes on these grounds until the late 1990s.

It was close to sunset.

"Look," I said, pointing. We saw what at first looked like a cat or a bobcat in a landscaped plot containing shrubs and azaleas, but when it sat on its haunches, we saw the tiny wrinkled face and the fur muff of the rhesus monkey. I remembered there had been a sign near the entrance warning visitors to not feed them. The monkey stared back at us without an ounce of fear or curiosity.

"Look," Bob said, pointing. "There's a little baby one out there."

I followed the direction of his finger and then sensed movement across the field. We looked—then we stopped pointing. I clutched Bob as four more monkeys loped into view. I whirled around and saw palm fronds shaking as another monkey shimmied up a tree. I whirled around again, and more monkeys were congregating in the field. We stood there, silently watching, as the simians crept out onto the landscaped grass and the sidewalks, brazenly staring at us. A few climbed palm trees, perhaps claiming them for the night.

"There's what," Bob said, "twenty, thirty, forty of them, maybe. Fifty?"

The number of monkeys kept climbing, now looking like a herd to us. They ran across the grass and toward the trees. A few ran toward us down the sidewalk. We slowly backed off—we were outnumbered.

"Let's go," I said.

It was hard to turn around and walk away slowly. I looked over my shoulder once. The monkeys were still coming. Four of them actively followed us. Perhaps there was some invisible line they had learned not to cross, but I doubted it. We turned and ran.

Later, I learned that a bunch of rhesus monkeys ganged up on some tourists last spring and chased them back to the glass-bottomed boats. There were a few editorials in local newspapers about the herpes B virus these two hundred monkeys carried in habitat at Silver Springs. The primates were branching out everywhere in north central and northeast Florida. I remembered the one little monkey I saw in the hammock last spring, when I was paddling from Gores Landing, and I wondered when their population explosion would change from an oddity to a pestilence. Rhesus monkeys are notoriously bad-tempered.

It was getting dark by the time we made it to the lighted windows of the Silver Springs Café, where a meatloaf and mashed potato dinner awaited us. It quickly became clear that sixty-eight paddlers had not materialized for this trip; there were about twenty-four of us.

Silver Springs monkeys.

I was relieved, because, frankly, I could not see battling those narrow river bends with so little room to maneuver. It turned out that a major kayaking extravaganza, the fifth annual Florida Paddle Rendezvous hosted by The Villages Canoe & Kayak Club, had occurred at Silver Springs State Park less than a month ago. The event featured three heady days on several waterways, including Juniper Creek, the Ocklawaha River, Rainbow River and Silver River. The people who had paddled that trek, understandably, had not signed up for the Ocklawaha Odyssey. But at least half of the twenty-four people going on the Odyssey trip this year had gone the previous year.

After dinner, we met in a training room set up with folding chairs, a screen and a podium. There were pictures of Silver Springs State Park past and present, including shots of Johnny Weissmuller, the Olympic swimmer who played Tarzan in black-and-white movies in the 1930s and 1940s. There was also a life-size replica of the Creature from the Black Lagoon.

One of the most successful trilogies in film history, the three "Creature" films—*Creature from the Black Lagoon*, *Revenge of the Creature* and *The Creature Walks Among Us*—were made over a period of two years in the 1950s.

They were filmed mostly in Wakulla Springs and California, although park visitors might recognize Silver Springs in some of the shots. The "creature," Ricou Browning, who was filmed in all the underwater shots, was a Wakulla Springs lifeguard.

When we were all seated, Bill Richards stood at the podium and began speaking.

"This is our forty-eighth trip in our tenth year. And this is our lowest-attendance trip. Twenty-four paddlers versus sixty-eight paddlers—what we had last year—is bad for us, but really good for you guys."

We looked around. The room was small and seemed packed by two dozen people. Someone coughed. Richards introduced us to the staff: Larry from St. Augustine and Marie and Ron from Naples (not their real names). One staff member would always lead with his kayak in front of the pack, one would paddle in the middle and one would bring up the rear. They all had cool kayaks, especially Larry. He owned a cedar strip kayak he bought from a teacher who had built it with her mother in her garage.

Richards continued, "There's a race at Ray's tomorrow. Get in the weeds so you don't get run over. Take your time with that. Any questions?"

Bob raised his hand. "What's the current?"

Richards conferred with Larry, who answered, "About two or three miles an hour."

Bob said, "Then we don't have to paddle, do we?" He sat back with a satisfied smile that I would come to remember as ironic.

Larry said, "Ha, ha—I beg to differ." Everyone laughed.

Richards continued. "Now, we're going to have a presentation by Craig Lindauer. He is a park services specialist. He started as a volunteer in 2009, in Gainesville, and he's been here since 2015. He's been a great help to us in planning this, and we're fortunate to have him as a contact person and a person who takes care of all the little details."

Lindauer, a tall, reedy man in civilian clothes, stepped up to the podium. He said, "Something to talk about is how significant this place was to old Florida. Once upon a time this was one of the most visited attractions in Florida. You can see some of the memorabilia around this room, pictures of movie stars, celebrities, all kinds of people came through here. Silver Springs didn't become a state park until 2013."

I knew people—old people—who remembered going out on the glass-bottom boats as kids. I was grateful this place of beauty had survived.

Lindauer continued: "This land that we're sitting on was purchased by the state of Florida in 1993 for twenty million dollars. A lot of the land along the river had been purchased in the mid-'80s. Until 1991, there was nothing there until Marion County Public Schools opened the Silver River Museum. They just celebrated their twenty-fifth year."

Bob and I had been there. I remembered a giant quilt of Marion County tacked onto the museum wall. Afterward, we strolled in the nearby wood and came close to an adult doe that was peeking at us from behind foliage. Bob, as usual, picked up a few ticks.

Lindauer said, "The museum sees about ten thousand fourth, fifth graders a year, plus more students for their annual events. They've already had a whole generation of people go through their program, and now their kids are going to the museum. We have a really good partnership with the school board. But it wasn't until 2001 that the campground, the cabins, the ranger station, a lot of the facilities for Silver River State Park were built."

Compared to the explosion of theme parks in central Florida, it seemed the cultivation of this exquisite spot was fifty years behind the times. I turned my attention back to Lindauer, who continued:

"In 2010, Palace Entertainment—they have theme parks all over the country, and they managed the lease here for the private nature school part—tried to start getting out of their lease. In 2013, they appealed to the state parks, and the governor and the cabinet officially approved a change to their lease terms in exchange for about four million dollars to improve infrastructure and to get it ready to become a state park."

It sounded like a lot of money, but four million dollars is not a lot to restore aging infrastructure. There were still remnants of the old Silver Springs water park near the parking lot, and Bob, Jack and I had canoed past the crumbling jungle cruise attraction last winter.

Lindauer continued: "October 1, 2013, was set up as an arbitrary date for the turnover; the state park scrambled to get this open, and we did it under a state of construction. On that date, the whole Silver River State Park merged with this entrance, and it's all now Silver Springs State Park. The entire river, five miles give or take a few, is now inside the park boundaries. There's over four thousand acres of the park. Ray Wayside is owned by the department of transportation, but it's leased and managed by Marion County."

He cleared his throat. "We're kind of like the gateway for the Ocala National Forest. I don't know if you guys have been to parks like Wekiva Springs State Park?"

Bob and I raised our hands. That was in our neck of the woods.

Lindauer nodded. "Wekiva Springs is completely surrounded by development. Fortunately, Silver Springs State Park is surrounded by public lands, so that's why it's so cool that we have this place. We have visitors from all over the world who don't know anything about Florida, and we have a great opportunity to teach them what Florida is all about."

I was beginning to get the gist of the state park's position on Silver Springs State Park. It was a symbol as much as a historic landmark and a precious environmental conservation area.

Lindauer said, "Relative to your group, though, when this became a state park, for the first time ever, you could launch your canoe or your kayak here. Before, you had to go all the way down to Ray Wayside. The glass-bottomed boats are still here, of course. Do you all have any questions before I show you a short video?"

A man raised his hand. "So, the glass-bottomed boats—do they still operate every day?"

Lindauer nodded. "The boats run from about 10:00 a.m. until 4:30 p.m. Those have been running since the 1920s. These boats are the same ones from the 1960s."

The man asked, "Is there an admission charge?"

"The admission charge for the park covers whether you want to launch a canoe or a kayak or ride the glass-bottom boat." Lindauer looked around the room. Then, he turned on the video. It showed the Olympic swimmer Johnny Weissmuller churning river water in one of his famous sprints. There was synchronized swimming being performed by women wearing one-piece bathing suits, bathing caps and full makeup. Apparently, there used to be a diving board in the headsprings.

The park also used to be segregated, and in 1949, a park for African Americans opened on the river. It was called Paradise Park and served the same purpose as Butler Beach in St. Augustine and American Beach on Amelia Island—a way for black citizens to get near the water on a segregated strip of land as per Jim Crow laws.

When the presentation was over, I stepped into the restroom before returning to the primitive campground. A woman from our group was in there wiping her face and arms with paper towels. Bob and I walked back to the campground with her. Her name was Cathy, and she was from Atlanta. Cathy had driven down to Florida by herself with her kayak strapped on the roof. She also had the wherewithal to bring an LED headlight to locate the path. It was hardly necessary, though. The moon was full, low and bright.

After Bob and I brushed our teeth in the dark, swigged water from the canteen and spit into the scrub, we lay there at last on our first night, looking directly up at the almost full supermoon. Because the moon was so close to the earth, it was like a midnight sun when I woke at 12:30 a.m. to use the plastic shed a few yards away. Mindful of possible simian intruders, I cautiously crept back to our little tent. The roar of motorcycles lulled me, finally, to sleep.

10

SILVER SPRINGS STATE PARK TO GORES LANDING

December 2, 2017

In the deep glens where they lived, all things were older than man
and they hummed with mystery.
—Cormac McCarthy, The Road

When we woke up in the morning, the walls of our tent were soaking wet. We dried off everything as best we could with a towel. For December, it was unseasonably warm. The temperature only got down in the low fifties that night, and it was already climbing toward the high seventies, where it would hover all day.

That day, we were to paddle from Silver Springs State Park to Ray Wayside Park (six miles), have lunch and then paddle to Gores Landing (ten and a half miles). The itinerary cheerfully laid out our day:

> *If you didn't get a chance to paddle over the lovely head spring yesterday, be sure to start your morning with this breathtaking view! Today we'll be paddling the beautiful, clear, tree canopied Silver River, enjoying a nice down-stream push from the head spring. Keep an eye out for monkeys, cormorants, anhinga's, herons, and egrets, as well as a diversity of freshwater fish, turtles, and maybe even a manatee or two below the water's surface. Our lunch stop will be at Ray Wayside Landing, six miles downriver. After lunch, the Silver River merges into the Ocklawaha River, which we'll follow another 10 miles to our campsite for the night at Gores Landing, a Marion County park. The Ocklawaha is an old*

river, spreading and braided with a mile-wide valley. On some sections, 5 river miles may result in 7-8 paddling miles—more if you stop to investigate one of the many braids or side creeks. Despite the development, the Ocklawaha is home to more than 100 species of fish, 200 varieties of birds, and 300 different mammals.

This lengthy itinerary worried us not at all. What I *was* worried about was our tandem kayak arriving by the 9:00 a.m. launch time, but I'd already put in so many calls to Mike and Sheri O'Neal at the Ocklawaha Outpost over the past few days that I thought I'd refrain. Bob and I are early risers, so we got up; broke camp; carried our tent, sleeping bag, backpack and duffle bag to the yellow Penske truck; put our toothbrushes in our pockets and set out for the public restroom at the park, then for breakfast at the Silver Springs Café. It was 7:30 a.m. We were still operating outside of visiting hours—the park wouldn't open for a half-hour.

The springs had a layer of mist hovering above the crystal-clear water. Everything was damp and fresh-looking, and the air smelled sweet. The glass-bottom boats were lined up in their slips. Fortunately, there were no monkeys in sight.

Cormorants at Silver Springs.

Great blue heron on the Ocklawaha River.

We walked into the café and found an outlet to charge our phones. After a fine breakfast of scrambled eggs, sausage, grits and fruit, we got to know a few more of our fellow paddlers. Some folks had come alone, like Cathy, and some had come in pairs. There were paddlers from Sarasota, Pittsburgh, Daytona. Most had been on this trip the year before and numerous other trips with Paddle Florida or with other kayaking organizations. Bob and I blithely admitted that this was our first sustained amount of time on the river.

This was readily apparent to everyone by 8:00 a.m., when our tandem Old Town kayak arrived. It was red and looked bigger—and heavier—than I'd remembered it. One of the paddlers, Tom, said, "This is the only tandem we've got in the group." This gave me the first stab of misgivings about our choice of boat, but I gamely gave Sheri O'Neal my credit card for the kayak rental and cabin rental at the Ocklawaha Outpost the following night. Then, we all sat around on a picnic bench until close to 9:00 a.m., when Bill Richards said we could launch.

Even with as few as twenty-four people, the planning involved for a trip like this was daunting. The odds of anyone getting hurt or lost were low, but

White egret at Ray Wayside Landing.

you never know. It occurred to me that Bob and I were the least experienced pair on the entire trip.

Bill warned us again about the kayak race, which was to begin at Ray Wayside Park at 9:30 a.m. The racers would be paddling upstream, right in our faces. Bob and I carried our kayak to the launch, and I hopped in the front and grasped the heavy wooden paddle. Bob settled in the back, and someone pushed us into the water.

We were soon pretty far behind the pack of kayakers for two reasons: One, the tandem kayak was heavier than I remembered and, without a rudder, hard to steer; the other reason was that Bob wanted to stop at the springs and take pictures from the kayak of the three statues sixty feet underwater. We knew they were covered in algae from viewing them the night before, but we had no idea how hard it would be to position the unwieldly kayak to get a clear shot. Finally, we just gave up and paddled hard to catch up with the others. By the time we did, everyone was pointing to a gator, which was hard to see, because its color and texture camouflaged it on the log on which it was sunning. Finally, the gator plopped off the log and into the river. Everyone stopped taking pictures and moved on.

The edges of the slow, deep stream were lined by the flowers and leaves of aquatic plants. I recognized the purple ones as pickerelweed. The roots and deadheads looked like petrified game, and one in the middle of the river looked like a bird of prey, mouth agape. One of the "backwater" guides, Mary, who was clearly charged with the stragglers, pointed to the top of a tree where two red-bottomed monkeys frolicked. They didn't run away like the monkey I'd glimpsed the year before; in fact, the creatures just ignored us, shimmying up and down the trunk or working the branches hand over hand.

Mary also pointed to a green heron, which I'd never identified before. She explained that it is somewhat secretive. It was stocky with roundish wings, short yellowish-greenish legs and a thick neck drawn up against its body; its bill was long and stiletto-like.

Soon, our interlude with wildlife was over. Around that time, the race, which started at Ray Wayside Park, began to make an impact on us. People were furiously paddling upstream in kayaks, canoes and paddleboats, churning up the water, facing us headlong. Bob and I paddled hard to avoid them in our barge of a kayak.

We had the exact same Old Town kayak we had rented from the Ocklawaha Outpost when we paddled from Gores Landing to Eureka the previous year. But now, perhaps in contrast to the sleek kayaks of our fellow paddlers, our boat seemed unwieldly and heavy, although part of that was because of Bob's backpack. It contained his camera, sunblock, assorted hats, a tripod, an underwater camera and the entire map of the Ocklawaha that Bob H. Lee had sent us, laminated, color-coded and hole-punched into a black binder.

Bob and I labored on, going into the weeds, dodging racers. We were going downstream on the Silver River, and we worked hard, although the rest of the paddlers glided by, eventually disappearing around the bend.

By the time we got to Ray Wayside Park, the racing paddlers were catching up with us. We pulled into the long channel, framed by lily pads, that led to the park. Everyone else had started lunch, which consisted of iced tea, peanut butter–and–jelly sandwiches, chips, crackers, bananas and orange wedges. Bob and I used the restroom, ate a few crackers and chatted with a few paddlers. Gary said we should be finished and setting up camp at Gores Landing by 2:00 p.m. We were back in the water by 11:45 a.m.

Bob and I continued our slow paddle along the river. There were many trees down—far more than when we'd paddled this stretch last year in our yellow kayaks. It was a swampy area, a tangled mass of weedy growth. There were gigantic palms and ancient cypress and live oak. In places, long beards of moss brushed the water's surface. Soon, we were in the very back of the pack. We had no way of knowing how far ahead the others were. With all the twists and turns in the river, they could be right ahead of us, and we wouldn't see them.

We kept looking for the bluff, the bench and little beach where we'd stopped last year to pick an orange off a tree and eat our lunch. After an hour and a half of paddling, we finally saw it, but we were not sure if it was the same place. The beach was submerged in water, many trees were down and the bench was on its side—evidence that Hurricane Irma had roared through. I could just see the trees shaken and uprooted by her mad invisible fist, could hear her shrieking, pistol-whipping wind until trees toppled in disarray, broken evidence of the fury and force of her elemental temperament.

The beach where the guys were partying last year was also empty, and a big "NO CAMPING" sign was plastered on a tree along the creek.

We kept trying to dodge fallen trees, and at one point, we glided headlong into the outstretched branches. One minute later, we were back on the river. Bob yelled, "A SPIDER!"

A huge banana spider was crawling up his leg. I tried to hit it with the paddle, and we started heading back into the branches. Bob deflected the

Downed tree after Hurricane Irma.

heavy oar and flicked the spider into the water. I started paddling again, trying to regain momentum.

Bob and I had never paddled sixteen and a half miles in a day. It was starting to seem onerous. My back and arms ached. We had to wear our life jackets, which restricted movement. We still couldn't see any of the other paddlers.

Still, around one bend, the reflection of a palmetto bush perfectly mirrored in the river water—as though the plant and its watery likeness were whole—was a sight as beautiful as any painting in an art gallery.

A walrus-shaped guy with a gray moustache zoomed past us on a jet ski.

I asked Bob, "How did he get through with all the downed trees?" Bob shrugged. Apparently, it wasn't too hard, because the jet-skier showed up again an hour later. We could hear him roaring around the bend, and then he was coming straight at us. My mouth opened to scream as I tried to paddle out of his way. The jet ski veered at the last minute and sent a huge wake into the kayak, splashing and soaking us. The guy yelled back at us, "I had to run it out." He was gone before we could ask him how far we were from Gores Landing.

Bob and I shook our heads like dogs. We were wet, as were our jeans, sneakers and shirts. Bob's camera was also wet. It took another day for it to dry out enough to use and then another day for a funny black border to disappear along the bottom and edges of the screen.

We looked for the red flag that Janice and Bill had promised would mark the launch of Gores Landing. We debated the time we left Ray and how many miles per hour we were going. This paddle was much harder than the one we took a year ago, because the water was high, and we had to keep zigzagging back and forth to avoid the branches of fallen trees. At one point, we again veered over to the shallow side to take a picture of yet another sunning gator. We almost went into the bush.

"That's dangerous," Bob said, recalling the warning the day before about "strainers." We could get caught on a tree down in the water, get sucked underneath, and get stuck in the underwater branches and not be able to get out. Of course, there wasn't much of a current, so that possibility seemed remote. But Bob, not taking any chances, got us out of there.

At a quarter to three, Bob said, "What's that?"

I looked through the gaps in the trees and saw land and what looked like a mobile home. I heard a dog bark. Then, on the left, I saw tents and the yellow Penske truck hauling our gear.

"We're here," I said.

"Where's the red flag?" Bob asked.

It was a few hundred yards downstream. We paddled to the launch, hopped out and pulled our clumsy tandem kayak parallel with the other kayaks. I feared we were embarrassingly behind. I even pictured Bill Richards saying, "This is obviously too much for you," and offering us a ride back to Silver Springs State Park.

It turned out that the group just ahead of us, the group we could not see because of the turns in the river, had just gotten there fifteen minutes before us. It was after 3:00 p.m.

"We hit a few snags," Cathy said, and she meant it—literally. Darryl, an accountant from Jacksonville, had a rudder on the back of his kayak that would not retract. So, they were stuck on a fallen tree for quite a while and had to get into the water to move the kayak.

It reassured me a little that Bob and I weren't the only ones who had trouble with that stretch of the river, although we did paddle in dead last and soaking wet. But Bill Richards was sitting in a lawn chair by the launch, and he said nothing about our drowned-rat appearance or about sending us back to Silver Springs. Instead, we talked about the viewing that night of Matt

Liz and paddlers at Gores Landing (note the black border from Bob's soaked camera).

Keene's film *Lost Springs*. Bill was surprised to hear we'd already seen it. "Not many people have," he said.

"In Jacksonville," I said. "At MOCA [Museum of Contemporary Art]."

Just then, I saw Matt Keene walking toward us as if on cue. He wore a bandana and had a dog on a leash. "This is Lily," he said. Lily was a Dutch Shepherd and wore a matching bandana.

Matt was camping at Gores Landing for the night so he could show his *Lost Springs* film and give a talk about it. Matt earned a living in the St. Johns County School District as an instructional television specialist. He was also the consummate expert on everything about Florida rivers and paddling. He was honored in 2015 as St. Johns Riverkeeper's Advocate of the Year. In 2015, he paddled the entire Ocklawaha River with a friend, Ryan Cantey.

On day one of their seven-day trip, they started at Haines Creek in the Lake Harris Chain of Lakes and paddled north, around seventy miles downstream, until they reached the St. Johns River. They finished at the Welaka Boat Ramp.

There was a major snag. When they reached the Rodman dam, they had to portage over the dam in order to continue along the historic river. That meant carrying two sixteen-foot-plus touring kayaks, along with gear and food, up and over the earthen berm and down to the boat ramp at the far side of the spillway.

Ryan and Matt both paddled homemade wooden Chesapeake Light Craft touring kayaks. The kayak Matt had was the same one he had used to paddle the length of the St. Johns River (310 miles) and all the way around the state on the Florida Circumnavigational Saltwater Paddling Trail (1,515 miles).

I had related our goals to Matt through email and how we planned to avoid the upper Ocklawaha. Matt said,

> *One thing most people aren't aware of about the Ocklawaha is how unique and pleasant the upper Ocklawaha is, upstream of the Silver River. Since the majority of the Ocklawaha's flow comes from the Silver River, there is a lot of focus on the Ocklawaha downstream from the Silver River. The upper Ocklawaha does not get much activity or attention but is an enjoyable, gentle paddle. This portion of the river spills out of a chain of lakes that once fed water to the Ocklawaha all the way from the Green Swamp. This part of the river and the state still has a lot of elements of "old Florida," the spring fed wilderness of the middle and lower Ocklawaha.*

I told Matt I was looking forward to seeing his film again, but first, Bob and I had to get out of our wet clothes. Gores Landing, mercifully, was not a totally primitive campground. Located in Fort McCoy in northeast Marion County, it offers a boat ramp, picnic tables and bearproof trash cans on the Ocklawaha River. It's state-owned property and is leased to the Marion County Board of County Commissioners, who have managed the facility since 1966. Although it advertises "primitive camping," there are real bathrooms with running water.

Everyone else already had their tents up, so Bob and I hurriedly set up under a palm tree. Inside our tent, we changed out of our wet clothes—our only clothes-change for the trip—and balled up the damp items in a plastic bag. The following night, we would be at the Ocklawaha Outpost. Maybe we could find a clothes dryer then.

So, clearly, it's not like we were really roughing it in the wilderness. That night, I got to see how a catering system worked in the middle of nowhere. The Ocklawaha itinerary claimed, "Meals will be provided by professional caterers or local civic groups. Expect hearty, hot fare for breakfast and dinner."

Rachel, the caterer, and her daughter pulled up in a Dodge truck and unloaded portable tables, large foil-covered aluminum trays, a huge bowl of salad, cookies and a small keg of iced tea. That night, they served chicken-fried steak with biscuits and gravy. Every meal also included a meatless entrée for the vegetarians on the trip.

Afterward, we all unfolded portable chairs and watched *Lost Springs* under the starry, temperate December sky and the luminous supermoon. Matt Keene then gave a short talk:

> *So it was March, we're paddling the Ocklawaha—me and Ryan Cantey, who I paddled the St. Johns River with—and we're at the tail end of one of these drawdowns, so the dam has been closed, the water's coming back up, and it's a normal paddling trip on a beautiful wild river. Then, we get to where the drowned forest is, where the impoundment starts—this'll be two days from now for y'all—and the water levels are still low enough that you can see the drowned forest.*
>
> *And the drowned forest was the area that was gutted during the impoundment. They came through with this machine called the tree crusher and other methods to clear acres of floodplain forest. What happens with the impoundment—it's at an eighteen-foot level, so the higher the water level of the impoundment, the more thousands of acres are currently being flooded. We're paddling through this area, we're seeing this drowned forest, and it probably was the biggest influence I experienced, the biggest environmental motivation. It was just so drastic to see the slime across the water and above the water where the trees were just basically rotting off.*
>
> *There are many springs along the Ocklawaha River impacted by the dam. Some are flooded by the impoundment, but even the springs upriver are stressed because of the inability of native migrating species to reach them. For instance, a manatee foraging along the Silver River run would provide tremendous benefit to Silver Springs and the Silver River in terms of managing aquatic vegetation, providing warm-water winter habitat and in terms of ecotourism benefit to the local community.*
>
> *I did a documentary project on that topic called* River Be Damned. *I started working on the* Lost Springs *film with the artist Margaret Tolbert prior to the 2015 drawdown. Margaret approached me based on my previous short documentary. And she asked me about going back during the drawdown and filming that environment again and looking at it through*

the springs. The dam in its normal operation, of holding back all this water, floods the "lost" springs, and when the water is released, the springs automatically come back to life.

I was immediately drawn to the project because of the powerful impact the drawdown had on me, and her idea of following a group of travelers visiting these transient springs was intriguing. The film took a little more than two years to finish.

I raised my hand. "Do you have any plans for a wider distribution of the film?"

Matt nodded and said, "We're waiting to hear back on film festival submissions, which will be coming in over the next five months. Acceptance to festivals shapes a wider release of the documentary. We have several screenings currently scheduled through spring of 2018. After the regional screenings and festival dates, we'll release a public link for the film so that it can be watched freely and hopefully used in restoration efforts."

I noticed that Natalie had cleaned up her catering tables, packed up and left, but there were still some cookies, crackers and tea. Janice said coffee would be ready at 7:30 the next morning.

That seemed like a long time to wait, and the night stretched out before us. Bob and I took advantage of the running water to sponge off and brush our teeth in a real bathroom. Then, we crawled into our damp tent, drew the thirty-year-old comforter over us and stared up at the moon, a moon unusually close to Earth, close enough to affect the human body, which, with it being about 75 percent water, made me wonder whether there weren't tides or currents at work inside of all of us in synchronicity with the river lapping a few feet away.

11

GORES LANDING
TO OCKLAWAHA OUTPOST

December 3, 2017

Don't quit. Suffer now and live the rest of your life as a champion.
—Muhammad Ali

When we awoke, the walls of the tent, the sleeping bag and most of our clothes were soaking wet. We emerged, in the near-dark, looking for coffee, but all we found were a couple of people doing yoga. It was early, barely 7:00 a.m., and there was a half-hour to wait for that coffee.

Bob and I picked out our driest clothes and packed up the tent and sleeping bag and put it in the yellow Penske truck along with Bob's backpack, which we hoped would lighten the kayak load. Bob went down to the river to cast a few lines, and I retained a chair so I could read for a half-hour. The book I was reading is one I would recommend for anyone bearing up under any kind of physical endurance event: *Follow the River* by James Alexander Thom.

The book is part-documentary, part-imagination, and it is based on a true story that took place in the mid-eighteenth century. Mary Ingles, a pregnant twenty-three-year-old woman, was captured by Indians on a summer day in Virginia and taken to a Shawnee settlement in Ohio. She escaped and headed toward home. Home was one thousand miles away. She slept on the ground, climbed up and down mountains and lived on roots and acorns—when she could find them. By the time she made it home on foot, naked, emaciated and covered with sores and lice, it was winter.

She survived and lived to be eighty years old. It seemed to me that a little bit of difficulty paddling a bulky kayak—or sleeping in a wet tent, for that matter—was not so bad in comparison to the plight of Mary Ingles.

After reading about Mary's meal of slugs, I put away my book and reread the printed itinerary for the day:

> *From Gores Landing, we paddle 9.5 miles to Eureka Boat Ramp, another Marion County park. Since this is a short day, lunch will be provided there. Eureka is the first part of the Ocklawaha where paddlers will see the Rodman Pool backing up the river, as much of the current becomes imperceptible in this stretch. You'll also be able to imagine what the Ocklawaha looked like before humans intervened with massive engineering projects. You will see cooters, sliders, alligators, water birds, ducks, and forest birds. Some people may be surprised to see that fall colors DO come to Florida, at least in this northern part of the state. As you float downriver, you should see some oranges and yellows hues among the cypress trees. Tonight's campsite at Ocklawaha Outpost will bring us a little closer to civilization as we'll have access to hot showers.*

Yet, in the end, even the prospect of sleeping in one of the Ocklawaha Outpost's cabins, something I had been longing to do for over a year, did not help during our worst day on the river.

The paddle from Gores Landing to the Ocklawaha Outpost was the hardest one for me and Bob. This is ironic, considering it was the shortest distance by kayak during the entire trip. It was ironic because Bob and I paddled the identical route in the same kind of kayak the year before. But there were so many trees down along the route, which required so much maneuvering with our clumsy rudderless kayak, that by mile five, I was uncomfortable. I took little pleasure in the blooming sprays of wild aster or even in the sight of a single beautiful white iris bloom almost hidden in swampy soil. All of Bob's pictures were fringed with that weird black border from the soaking his camera received the previous day, and we wondered if it would ever work correctly again.

For December, it was uncommonly warm during the day, even under the canopy of cypress. Each stroke of the paddle was an effort, and only two things sustained me. One was the knowledge that I would sleep in a real bed in a real cabin that night—not just a "primitive" cabin, but one with hot running water. The other was a passage I'd just read in *Follow the River* that involved Mary Ingles singlehandedly launching a dugout

Above: Cabin at Ocklawaha Canoe Outpost and Resort in Fort McCoy.

Opposite: Climbing aster downstream on the Ocklawaha River.

Indian canoe into rushing river water. The canoe sank. She could not swim. And so on.

By the time Bob and I saw the bridge and the sign for the Ocklawaha Outpost, we felt as though we'd made it to the Emerald City, almost literally, as the river launch is mirrored by the overhanging green boughs of ancient trees.

Lunch was waiting for us, and Bill or Janice had put out some old bumper stickers, ours for the taking, with the words "SAVE THE OCKLAWAHA RIVER." More recent FDE bumper stickers replaced "SAVE" with "RESTORE," which did not carry quite the same impact according to Jack Bass, who'd been looking for an old one to put on the back of his Ram truck.

Our cabin was a prefab—250 square feet with a screened porch, a loft, a king-size bed, a tiny bathroom and two bunk beds. There was heat and air and even a TV. Mary Ingles never had it so good.

Sheri O'Neal, the proprietor, had a lending library in a small outbuilding with a pay washer and dryer. Bob and I stuffed our wet clothes into the dryer, fed coins into it and walked up to the convenience store for a soda and a bottle of Tylenol. When we returned, I sat on a picnic bench on the screened-in porch and read *Follow the River* until our clothes were dry.

Our fellow paddlers ambled by now and then with a friendly wave, but the afternoon was quiet. Bob took a nap in the cabin, then watched a basketball game for an hour. The sun set.

The moon was abnormally large and low that night, even for a supermoon, and we ate lasagna, salad, banana pudding and peach cobbler under its lunar glow. Captain Karen Chadwick, one of the creators of the Ocklawaha Odyssey route and the Santa Fe Audubon Society's 2018 Conservationist of the Year, was set to present a slideshow that night with pictures from the 2016 trip. On the table before her were gleaming blocks of what looked like quartz. As she talked, it became clear to me that the route we were paddling had an ancient perspective.

"Come on up here and see these and hold these," she said.

Bob asked, "And what's that?"

"This is a mastodon tooth." She placed her hand on a huge block of fossilized plaque. Mastodon means "nipple tooth"—so called because of the shape of the mastodon's molar teeth. The mastodon is an ancient elephant and a distant relative of the woolly mammoth. The tooth we were handling could have been over ten or fifteen thousand years old.

"You found this on the Ocklawaha?" I asked. Apparently, the rivers were rife with prehistoric bones. Archeologist Mike Stallings had recently made the front page of the *Palatka Daily News* in an article titled "Down to the Bone." The story was about a mastodon shoulder Stallings found while diving in the St. Johns River near Drayton Island.

Captain Karen shrugged. "At Silver Springs, about halfway down the Silver River? There's another dig there. This is a lower right-side molar." She held up another sheath of bone. "This is a mastodon patella, a kneecap, found in the Ocklawaha, upstream from here, a place you already went by."

She showed a slide of an old map and began an abbreviated history of the Ocklawaha:

> The Treaty of Moultrie Creek was signed in 1823. The Seminoles, composed of several different tribes, retained the interior. It was rough land, it was swampy, hard to get around. They relinquished the coastline to the white skippers who wanted it to navigate around the peninsula. One of the problems with the treaty was that the Seminole tribe was a refuge for escaped slaves who married into the tribe. The treaty dictated that escaped slaves had to be returned to their owners, and if the Indians moved out west, the former slaves, which were now family, had to go back to enforced servitude.

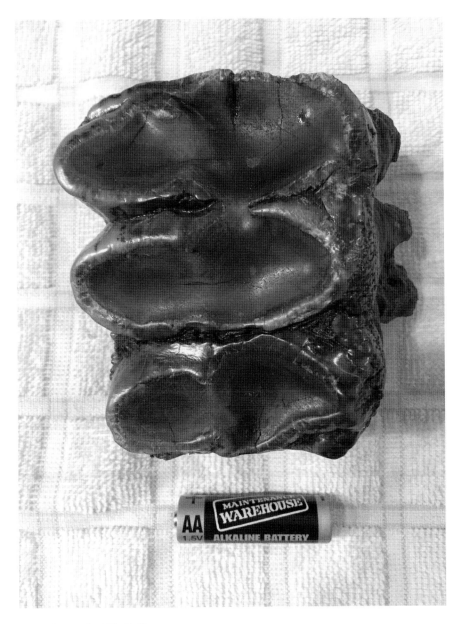

Mastodon tooth. *Mike Stallings*.

On Payne's Landing, where you're going tomorrow, there was another proposed treaty in 1832. Jackson and Congress put together the Indian Removal Act to relocate native Americans out west. The chiefs did not want their people to go. The politicians said, "Well, you signed a treaty." The Indians claimed their signatures were a forgery, but the government was unmoved. They said, "You've got three years to move." That started the second Seminole War, and a lot of Seminoles started migrating down to the Everglades.

She stopped and looked around. "By the late nineteenth century, Eureka, where we are, was one of the paddleboat stops for Colonel Hubbard Hart. So was the place you're going tomorrow: Orange Springs." I remembered Jack Bass saying there used to be a ferry there that he and his grandfather would take to their camp. His grandfather abandoned the camp after the dam blocked the river.

As if she were following my thoughts, abruptly, without a segue, Captain Karen clicked the slideshow into motion. A picture of an earthen dam was on display—Rodman dam.

Captain Karen said, "That's the dam."

Someone said, "That's the damn dam."

I swatted at a mosquito, alive and well in December. At least there were no ticks—as yet.

Bill interjected, "We're going to finish about a mile from there."

Using a laser pointer, Captain Karen said, "You'll see it from the other side. This is the downstream side. These are the gates to let the water out. When Irma came through, this gap here was five feet. And that water was just roiling out there."

She paused. "They'd [Army Corps of Engineers] given the dam a life span of fifty years. And next year, it'll be fifty years old. It's got a lot of damage. They did an inspection in 2016 and found the dam and the locks need two million dollars' worth of repairs. There's a lot of cracking in the concrete. There're holes underwater. It's rusty, the hydraulics are leaking. You know, it's reaching the end of its lifespan."

I had read about the dam's deterioration in an online report commissioned by the Department of Environmental Protection in 2015 and titled "Kirkpatrick Dam and Spillway Condition Assessment." I had seen the rust and cracks with my own eyes. The irony is that the Ocklawaha River restoration is a relatively inexpensive project because of the low cost of breaching the dam. In contrast, the maintenance costs for the dam top out at $1 million annually based on a study prepared twenty years ago by the St. Johns River Water Management District. In any case, the current situation is not sustainable. There is inadequate funding allocated to safely maintain the current structure, and there are no funds assigned for an alternate setup.

Captain Karen continued, "And because of the dam, the manatees can't migrate up freely from the St. Johns up into the Ocklawaha without going through the locks. The locks are open three days a week, fifteen minutes in the morning, fifteen minutes in the afternoon." She was referring to the Buckman Locks in the Cross-Florida Barge Canal south of Palatka.

She clicked again and showed a map. "This is an emergency plan that is not well known or made public. If the dam did fail? There are parts of Welaka that could flood."

What I remembered of Welaka was a big bluff, so flooding did not sound as dire as it otherwise might have. But I was reminded of another leaky Florida dam, the Okeechobee, and the fate of the Glades area if it ever breached. All the water there is being held back by a troubled earthen dike that surrounds the lake. After strong storms, it could collapse, and that would be the end of southeast Palm Beach County.

Bill said, "Tell them where Welaka is and where this is." Then he proceeded to tell us himself. "So, this river is dammed right here, and if you go on the other side of it, it continues thirteen miles to the St. Johns River." Bob and I nodded. We made that exact trip in Bob H. Lee's boat. "And a mile across the St. Johns River is the town of Welaka."

Captain Karen said, "And the Ocklawaha is right opposite that town. It's a high bluff there, but the low areas would get flooded. Congressman Ted Yoho has a house there."

The slide clicked again, and the screen showed Cannon Springs. "So, this is what the dam is doing to Cannon Springs." The slide displayed tannic-colored water. "During the drawdown, the spring is crystal clear. This is what it looks like now. I don't know why Marion County commissioners don't think this"—she clicked on a picture of gin-colored water—"is more of an asset"—she clicked back to the tannic water—"than this."

The path to Cannon Springs was under a leafy canopy of trees toward a pool of water. Twice, I had watched Margaret Ross Tolbert kayak down that picturesque side creek in a film. The fact that few outside of the small circle present knew about it made it even more alluring.

Captain Karen showed us a series of slides representing high water lines along the river prior to and during the drawdown of the dam to show how much land is unnecessarily flooded. She said:

Barge canal off Highway 19 east to Buckman Lock.

About nine thousand acres. That's a lot of wildlife habitat for bears and birds. When you get down past Eureka, you'll really see a difference. There's just no shoreline at all. The water is going way back into the woods. You'll see alligators and wading birds, wild turkeys. You'll see all kinds of tracks on the muddy banks, even hog prints. What's normal is water about three to four feet lower. The water is much clearer during the drawdown because it's mostly fed with spring water.

She pointed to a map on the screen, "Upriver from Cannon Springs is a place called Fiddia's Landing. And that is where Marjorie Kinnan Rawlings stayed with the Fiddia family when she was doing research for *South Moon Under*, which came out in 1933. She stayed with that family there to figure out how scrub crackers lived."

I remembered that book, and it's another tome I'd recommend for an endurance event. It details the social get-togethers in the scrub that featured moonshine, lard cake and roasted squirrel heads. There are many harrowing passages, including a logjam during a hurricane.

Captain Karen said, "The Fiddias were just eking out a living. They had a moonshine still, and they were trying to sell moonshine, you know, to keep alive. They hunted deer, they shot limpkin illegally and ate it, and Rawlings helped to run the still. So, that's where her research came from."

Afterward, Bob and I walked back to our cabin, brushed our teeth, took a hot shower and lay down in a real bed. I read for a while about Mary Ingles climbing an icy mountain inch by inch. Then I lay on my back staring at the ceiling, listening to Bob's even breathing.

I didn't kid myself. Endurance was not the same as momentum. I wondered if I would make it through the next two days.

12

OCKLAWAHA OUTPOST TO ORANGE SPRINGS BOAT RAMP

December 4, 2017

> *There is always the need to carry on.*
> —*Marjorie Stoneman Douglas*

FROM THE OCKLAWAHA ODYSSEY ITINERARY:

> *From the Eureka Boat Ramp, we paddle 13.2 miles to Orange Springs Boat Ramp, after a lunch stop at Payne's Landing (7.5 miles). In this section the river basin widens out and, in many stretches, becomes more clogged with vegetation. During these periods some of the small springs can be seen and many "islands" appear on the northern stretch.*

It was only seven and a half miles to Payne's Landing for lunch and six miles to the Orange Springs campground, which was "primitive" like the first one we stayed at in Silver Springs State Park—no running water.

Breakfast was quiche (sausage or spinach). Walking down to the kayak launch, I noticed two of the paddlers discreetly dropping out—carrying their kayak up the small incline to the yellow truck and a ride back to Silver Springs. I nudged Bob.

"I see that," he said.

It was tempting to follow their example, and later, Bob said he felt the same. It would be so easy for us, too. After all, we'd rented the kayak from the Ocklawaha Outpost—we could just leave it here. Then I thought of Mary Ingles, spitting teeth into her cupped hand as she crawled on her hands and knees across a frozen cornfield. I realized I could and would finish the trip.

It turned out that my apprehension about an untenable day on the water was groundless. First, this was a part of the river that Bob and I had never seen. By turning left at the outpost instead of right, we entered the backed-up water of the reservoir. We stopped to study the pilings for barges that never came behind Eureka dam, which was built and never used. The structure remains a colossal abandoned ruin.

When we commenced paddling toward Payne's Landing, the water was broad and beautiful. An eagle perched on a skeletal tree. There were no downed trees and no detours, and the water lettuce—unlike what Mike O'Neal described the previous year—was not too bad this season.

Larry, the paramedic from St. Johns County, was assigned to the stragglers, which consisted of me and Bob and Steve and Darren, a son-in-law/father-in-law duo from Sarasota. Steve was bass fishing, trailing a line out of the back of his kayak. The whole mood of this paddle was slower-paced than the day before. Bob's camera had finally dried out, and he could take pictures without the black border displaying. Larry was a genial guy who waited for Bob to finish taking pictures or for Steve to adjust his bass lures. He even took us down the tree-lined canal to Cannon Springs, which I recognized from Matt's film. Cannon Springs was a beautiful swimming spot—albeit a stagnant, tannic-colored one because of the weight of flooded water.

Larry told us that four paddlers had dropped out, not just two. "It happens every year," he said. "For some, the exertion required is more than expected, or it's not what they thought it would be. But not too many do that."

I said nothing about how close Bob and I had come to quitting. I was very glad I hadn't, because despite the ache in my back, arms and shoulders, the novelty of this stretch of the river was exhilarating. Our path was an eerie yet beautiful landscape lined with channel markers because of the stumps of cypress trees downed by the old tree crusher and drowned by the reservoir fifty years back. We began to see some bass fishing boats marked by the color and pattern of camouflage; the boaters also wore camouflage.

Since our kayak could not be damaged much by a run-in with a stump, Bob charted a straight line outside the channel markers, which was shorter in distance, and the effort of paddling seemed much less than during the previous two days, even when Larry said, "Let's catch up."

We dug in and made it—late—for lunch. Stopping at Payne's Landing was cancelled because of some obstruction, so we met on the other side,

Canal lock at Eureka.

Dock to lock at Eureka.

in a sandy knoll, and ate peanut butter–and–jelly sandwiches and oranges unloaded from Janice's van. After eating, some paddlers disappeared into the woods, then came back out, but our entire stop was no longer than fifteen minutes. We were urged back into our kayaks for the final paddle of the day into Orange Springs.

Payne's Landing to Orange Springs consisted of flooded standing timber and areas of floating vegetation. Larry continued to hang back, bringing up the rear with Bob, Steve, Darren and me. We were grateful to have a paramedic along. Bob asked, "Does anyone ever get hurt?"

Larry said, "No." Then he said, "Last year, someone fell out of the boat on the last day because of all the water lettuce, but she just ended up getting a ride in the airboat."

Lucky, I thought. Tomorrow, we would paddle across the reservoir, and last year the weather had been bad and the way choked with vegetation. An airboat led the way, clearing the path, but it was rough going, from what I'd heard from Cathy, who'd paddled the Odyssey the year before.

I stared straight ahead at the vista. I could see why the last leg of the trip had to be across the reservoir; it was an awakening to the reality of the river's dilemma. In front of us, wood ducks and cormorants made off at angles from our paddling course. The cool breeze in my face felt good.

Then, Steve caught a bass. We cheered. Around that time, we saw Mary waiting in a kayak with an orange flag hoisted to usher us into the Orange Springs campground. Steve stayed behind to fish, and we paddled up the boat launch. It had been a glorious ride.

While I was unloading our gear from the yellow truck, one of the paddlers, Jim, asked me, "Any running water here?"

"Not that I know of," I said, although there were brand-new porta-potties.

He smiled, ruefully, and rubbed his chin. "I wanted to clean up before I got home. Not look like I've been roughing it."

"You have." I said, "Been roughing it." Jim, like most of the paddlers, was in his fifties or sixties, retired from—or holding—a steady, responsible job.

A lot of people on the trip—in fact, most—had come solo or with a buddy, not a spouse. The Ocklawaha Odyssey was a good way to indulge a favorite pastime with likeminded people, even if a partner wasn't into it. And what do they say about absence and the heart?

"Well," Jim said, walking off, "I know she'll love me anyway."

Orange Springs used to be a popular tourism spot in northern Marion County until after the Civil War, when Silver Springs became a common steamboat destination. It was still a spot for annual fishing tournaments. A sign directed anglers to weigh their bass before releasing them. The daily bag limit was five fish.

We saw a bass fisherman on his way out, standing in his boat.

"Do any good?" Bob asked.

"Fifty bass. Biggest, six pounds." We didn't ask, but it must have been catch and release.

We saw bass fishermen headed into the water, in boats, tinkering fruitlessly with outboard motors. I heard one would-be angler say to another, "Get over here and see can you start this motha."

What Orange Springs was not was a regular campground, and Paddle Florida got permission to use it for the Odyssey. It was tree-lined, abutting the water—shady yet full of light.

Bob and I put up our tent and went for a long walk. The paved road was just wide enough to avoid the woods and foil the ticks' penchant for Bob. The air smelled sweet, the way it does if you are many miles away from a city.

Later, everyone lounged in camp chairs by their tents and watched the sun go down. Orange Springs is a particularly pretty spot, with a glossy cove

Camping at Orange Springs.

that reflected all the colors of the sinking sun. Paddlers stopped by the tents to chat. One paddler had hooked up a portable outdoor shower and invited everyone to stop by and use it.

Dinner that night was teriyaki chicken or vegetables, and dessert was brownies. The moon rose, penetrating the water, and I imagined fish gliding beneath the surface. A local band played bluegrass, but the breeze barely moved enough to be felt, and mosquitos were coming out, so Bob and I listened from inside our tent. I finished *Follow the River.* Mary Ingles made it home to Virginia, reunited with her husband and had four more children. Her happy ending boded well for the rest of the trip, which would conclude the next afternoon.

13

ORANGE SPRINGS BOAT RAMP TO RODMAN DAM

December 5, 2017

This, then is the Ocklawaha Wilderness area of Central Florida…
this valuable complex of wilderness, which, mostly by plain good luck,
remains a sample of the original Florida.
—Marjorie Harris Carr

FROM THE OCKLAWAHA ODYSSEY ITINERARY:

We'll paddle the final 6.7 miles to Rodman Campground where we'll see
firsthand the severing of the Ocklawaha River by the infamous George
Kirkpatrick Dam at Rodman Reservoir. For the last 2.5 miles our paddle is
in reservoir (called Lake Ocklawaha). Here the ghostly remains of dead tree
tops appear both above and just below the water surface, left over from the
creation of the reservoir. You have to keep a sharp lookout to prevent running
up on them, especially if it's windy.

That night I was awakened by fierce vocalizations from what sounded like a nearby owl. There were no hoots, but there were screams, screeches and shrieks. I had no desire to get in the middle of whatever was occurring outside our tent, but I did not go back to sleep, even after the sounds ceased. I reflected that the owl was the symbol of the goddess Athena in Greek mythology, a goddess of wisdom and of prophecy. I unzipped our humid tent in time to see the sun assemble itself over the water, which then filled with light, illuminating aquatic life moving in errant flotation.

After a breakfast of oatmeal, we embarked on the end of our journey. To get to the Rodman dam required navigating the river channel and the Rodman Reservoir (also called a lake and a pool). Along the way were floating vegetation (hydrilla and eelgrass), dead standing trees and underwater trees and stumps. Water depths were down to thirty feet. There was no current.

Referred to as "Florida's Pompeii" by Lars Anderson (an author and environmentalist and the owner and river guide of Adventure Outpost), Rodman Lake wasn't the most beautiful leg of our trip, but it was one of the most important. I realized this as I spent my fourth day on the water and when the enormity of the close shave the Ocklawaha had with extinction finally dawned on me. If it weren't for Marjorie Harris Carr and the Florida Defenders of the Environment (FDE), the entire Ocklawaha River could look like Rodman Lake.

When the reservoir was built, the U.S. Army Corps of Engineers dug a straight channel to accommodate heavy barges. The trees that were left died and decayed, except for their stumps, which were revealed during drawdowns. Anyone who had been on the reservoir during a drawdown could see that the Ocklawaha River channel was unbroken. Yet, anyone

Rodman Reservoir tree stumps.

Beginning our paddle on Rodman Reservoir.

could also see that open standing water, tannic-colored and acidic, was clearly not the same as a healthy river and a floodplain swamp.

This wasn't the first time I saw Rodman Lake, but it was the first time I paddled across a short portion of its vast exterior, approximately fifteen miles in length. It was easy for me to see beneath the obvious and imagine what was. I saw what it could have been if not for the catastrophe of the Cross-Florida Barge Canal. I could see the far shore, with a distant line of living trees fringed in haze. But in 1872, at the beginning of the paddle wheeler era, this area with the flat water and clumps of hydrilla and floating stumps would have been a vast riverine swamp, wild and free with hidden bubbling springs and ancient cypress. I imagined steam-driven vessels filled with northerners on what was then a four-day jungle adventure from Palatka to Silver Springs and back. And then, my mind drifted back in time to the 1600s or before, when the white man hadn't yet made an appearance, and the only craft sailed through these waters was a hand-fashioned dugout canoe. Natives camped on the shore and dug for roots.

Last day of the Ocklawaha Odyssey—crossing Rodman Reservoir.

As usual, Bob and I lagged in the rear with our tandem Old Town kayak. Darren forged ahead, saying, "Let's get this done." I could see the rest of our paddling party miles in the distance, sort of the way you can see the Washington Monument from any part of the vast National Mall. The sun beat down on us. An osprey hovered, and I recalled that I'd read that Audubon volunteers constructed poles for their nests near Rodman preserve in the upper portion of the lake.

It took two and a half hours to make it to the Rodman campground, and we pulled up in a sludge of hydrilla. Everyone was all business, stacking kayaks on top of the shuttle back to Silver Springs. Our own borrowed kayak was picked up by Ocklawaha Outpost within minutes.

We ate barbeque in a pavilion shaded from the hot sun that burned my face and earlobes in spite of my baseball cap. Bob and I ran into Donnie Adams, who was there to help transport kayaks back to the state park. We ate lunch with him and listened to an FDE member promote the Silver Ocklawaha Blueway Action Plan, which would provide a path through the Rodman dam to the lower Ocklawaha leading to Palatka and the mouth of the St. Johns River.

"What do you think?" I asked Donnie.

"If anything good can happen, it will," he said, optimistically.

Drivers from Silver Springs showed up to take us back to the park. We said goodbye to Janice and Bill and boarded. An hour later, Bob and I were actually in our own car with our gear stowed in our own car trunk. We said goodbye to our paddling companions and headed home. In the car, I looked at my phone messages for the first time in five days—nothing too urgent seemed to require my attention.

Bob and I had covered new terrain in our forty-five-mile paddling adventure on the Ocklawaha River. As with all adventures, the experience changed us, but we had yet to determine how.

14

ELECTROFISHING WITH THE FLORIDA FISH AND WILDLIFE CONSERVATION COMMISSION

June 15, 2018

You know when they have a fishing show on TV?
They catch the fish and then let it go. They don't want to eat the fish,
they just want to make it late for something.
—*Mitch Hedberg*

*Note: There were two FWC employees on this trip. For convenience, I have
depicted only one.

After our recreational Paddle Florida trip, Bob and I wanted to spend
some time with an agency tasked with the business of managing and
monitoring the Ocklawaha River. In June, Bob and I went with Ryan
Hamm, a Florida Fish and Wildlife Conservation Commission (FWC) fishery
administrator, to electroshock fish on the Ocklawaha River. The purpose
was to count sample species, a duty undertaken every spring by the FWC.

In terms of fish, the Ocklawaha is one of the most diverse rivers in
Florida, with sixty different species. There are five or six species of sunfish,
bluegill, bowfin, three or four types of darters and a couple of species of
shiners, although the bluenose shiner is rarely seen. The river is rife with
largemouth bass. Over the decades, some species of fish have declined,
while some have increased.

The striped bass disappeared upstream in the 1970s, and experts say that
had to do with the decrease in flow and higher water temperature created
by the Rodman dam. But the Florida Fish and Wildlife Conservation

Commission does not weigh in on the restoration of a free-flowing Ocklawaha River (although, according to the FDE, they prefer at least a partial restoration). Like the St. Johns River Water Management District, they are neutral on the issue.

But the health of the river and its surrounding wildlife is more than an avocation for FWC employees. It is a selfless career built on academic and practical knowledge, teamwork and a love of nature.

Bob and I arrived at Ray Wayside Landing at 9:30 a.m., a half-hour early for our appointed meeting time. The water was high, obscuring the dock. The water was also dark—a bad sign, because when the water gets dark, it kills off vegetation, which does not attract fish. Bob cast some new lures he'd purchased the night before. No bites.

Around 9:50 a.m. a four-wheel-drive pickup with a trailer and a boat pulled up. The truck had the FWC seal, and so did the custom johnboat, a Sea Arch, which bore the legend, "ELECTROFISHING: DANGER." On board was Hamm, a bearded, thirtyish man who paused from setting up the controls to shake hands with Bob and me. He provided blue life jackets, which we quickly shrugged on, and we were soon on our way.

Hamm was born in Okeechobee but grew up in the Midwest and went to school at Purdue, majoring in wildlife fisheries and management (the University of Florida offers a similar degree). He got a job with the FWC at the start of his career, thirteen years ago. He's worked primarily in north and central Florida and says that all FWC employees have a shared passion for fish and wildlife and their habitats.

On the Ocklawaha, he participates in long-term monitoring of water volume, which is consistently monitored every year, enabling the FWC to establish trends. "Today," he said, "one thing about our electrofishing, if we were to do our samples today? It would be incredibly biased. Our water is up, when it is normally much lower, so our catch rates today would not be comparable with last year or the year before that. This year is a bit of an anomaly. But over time, we can correct some of those environmental factors and answer the question of what the fish distribution is like out there."

In Florida, the wet season is summer. In the spring of 2018, it was very wet. So, the river was up at a time it would normally be much lower and when the fish community would typically concentrate in smaller areas. Hamm wasn't sure what FWC research would conclude about the widely dispersed fish and consequent samples from the day. He may have to go out again this summer and collect more samples under better conditions, provided they occur.

"Look at that brown cloud in the water," Bob said, pointing.

Florida Fish and Wildlife Conservation Commission electrofishing boat.

Hamm nodded. "When you come to this area, you get a crash course in thermodynamics, how the liquid moves and mixes."

That did not seem like a bad idea on a glorious spring day on the Ocklawaha. We motored down the channel, which was wide and full and devoid of the vegetation and fallen trees we'd seen in the past. We turned

Cormorant in Ocklawaha River habitat.

left at the end of the channel and began motoring downstream, under the bridge. Most of our familiar landmarks—stretches of hyacinths and spatterdock and banks of white sand—were under water. The spot where, over a year ago, the partying dudes yelled at me to row faster was flooded as high as the picnic table. We also passed herons, cormorants and wood ducks. A white egret flew overhead, and butterflies congregated along the banks. We saw a small gator and a cooter (softshell turtle) sharing a log.

"We've heard the limpkins are almost gone from the Wakulla River," I said. "But we've seen quite a few on the Ocklawaha."

"It's the apple snails [that limpkins feed on]," Hamm said. "They're gone from Wakulla, but we have some. We even have exotic apple snails. They're apple snails on steroids—they eat more, they leave more eggs."

As the national gateway for foreign plants and animals, Florida is home to several species of apple snails, with only one being native. The Florida Apple Snail is one of the smaller members of the genus and hasn't changed much in several million years. The exotic snails are probably from South America and started showing up in Lake Okeechobee in 1987, where they rapidly spread.

We passed under the Highway 40 bridge. The banks were so flooded that it was hard to recognize a waterway Bob and I had already kayaked at least a half-dozen times. Every time we were on the Ocklawaha River, it looked a little different. We saw an anhinga poke its skinny, snakelike neck out of the water, then disappear. After about half an hour motoring downstream, Hamm started to set up the boat for electrofishing.

The "electrofisher," a big silver box with six plugs coming out the back, acts like a diode. It is a semiconductor device with two terminals, typically allowing the flow of current in one direction only, from the metal "booms" (retracted while boating, pushed forward when electrofishing) in the water to the hull of the boat. From the box, the electricity passes down the conductor's wires at a particular gauge to handle the amperage the unit is expected to generate. Wires run in flexible watertight conduits, and the edges of the boat are padded. When the pedal, which is similar to a gas pedal, is pushed, it heightens the current. To efficiently run the box, and appropriately stun the fish, Hamm needs to know the conductivity of the water, the temperature of the water, the amount of dissolved oxygen in the water and pH salinity.

Bob said, "All those things are settings on the box? The fish don't have a chance."

Hamm replied, "Well, this is for data collection and sampling and for sheer curiosity. We want to know what's down there. We have a depth finder, sonar, fish finder, the whole nine yards. Another part of that long-term monitoring program is a river-mapping program. We use the depth finder and side-scan sonar to create a map of the river bottom and how it may change over time in terms of sediment thickness, sediment size, vegetation." Hamm continued working the box. "We're looking for a certain amperage so we can adjust the voltage, the voltage per second and a range. It creates an electric field."

Bob said, "I saw you had metal going down off the front of the boat like a skirt."

Hamm nodded. "The current goes out to the booms, zooms back to the boat, back out to the booms."

Electrofishing boat booms.

Hamm said we were at twenty-five feet of depth, which was too deep for catfish. I asked, "Do different fish react to the box differently?"

"Yes," Hamm said. "Catfish, because of the amount of taste buds and sensors all over their bodies, won't shock like a sport fish, like bass or bream. What we do is tickle them—six to nine amps for a decent stun. With a catfish, we take it down to one and a half amps with a very low pulse rate. It tickles them so bad, you will see literally hundreds of catfish start jumping out of the water all around the boat."

Such a sight would be tempting to poachers who can be overt in their wrongdoing. Bob talked about watching kids in Turkey throw dynamite in the water to catch fish. Then, there is the clever pillager who fine-tunes his crime. I thought back to what Bob H. Lee told us about the poacher Roger Gunter and his "monkey fishing" catfish apparatus, a five-bar Western Electric crank telephone rigged with an electric motor and a rheostat wire to rev the apparatus up or down. He illegally bagged thousands of catfish. I thought of all the people I had seen peacefully and respectfully fishing off the dam or in the side creeks in the river. As Bob H. Lee says, the job of the game warden is to ensure fairness between predator and prey. It's not a sport when there is a one-sided advantage.

Hamm, committed to monitoring health, abundance and locale of local fish species, continued, "Some fish are actually attracted to the field—mudfish, bass, tilapia. Other species feel that field coming, and they just disappear. Big fish don't get big by being dumb. We utilize other methods like trophy catching for sampling, where we measure, weigh and throw the catch back."

He sat back. "Ready to bring some fish up? Don't fall in. Especially when I fire up this box. It can kill you." He handed us two long poles. "Take that and put it up front. You guys are going to dip the fish. Pull them in with the net. Most of the fish that we shock are going to come up around the boom. So, basically, the field is going to be from here to out around five feet. The fish will come up; dip them out of the water, then put them in the tank behind us here. After we do that, we'll stop, and we'll have a look at the fish."

Bob and I positioned ourselves on either side. We each grabbed a net with a long pole. The electrofishing box came on with an electronic roar. Looking into the river water near the booms, I saw a small fish lying on its side right itself and dart off. I managed to dip a few fish, including one enormous bass. I found the long poles clumsy, heavy and hard to revert to drop the fish into the holding tank. Bob dipped a few more fish than I did.

Electrofishing bass sample.

Hamm turned off the electrofishing box and turned his attention to the fish in the holding tank. Some looked to be different sizes of the same species. The first was the largemouth bass, a creature weighing at least three pounds. It steadily eyed us as Hamm explained that Florida bass were a unique subspecies, genetically different than northern bass: "They grow faster, they reach larger sizes and they're actually less aggressive than northern bass when it comes to nest protection."

Hamm tossed the bass overboard. "Let this one live."

I looked into the water and saw the bass lying on its side. I asked, "Is he going to make it?"

"Oh yeah," Hamm said.

We saw some lily pads rustle—and not from the wind. Hamm withdrew his hand. "Water moccasin. It's mating season."

The bass revived and darted off. I wondered at the stealth of the moccasin to linger on the fringe of an event that immobilized potential prey. Not for the first time, I considered the depth of consciousness of water creatures.

Hamm said, "I would much rather deal with a gator than a moccasin."

I would prefer neither—a pesky afterthought about predators, always, amidst a day spent out in nature. While climbing a mountain in Colorado with my daughter, she turned to me and said, briskly, "If we spot a mountain lion, we're done."

Hamm netted a huge golden shiner. Hamm said, "Very important bait species in Florida. I would call this a three-dollar fish. If you were to buy a dozen of these and go bass fishing, probably cost you about forty dollars. These are really hardy, especially on a hook, and bass love to eat 'em." He tossed the shiner overboard, where, perhaps, it would get eaten by the bass Hamm had released moments ago.

Bob looked on longingly and listened closely. He had his preferred lures, but I could tell he was considering the shiner.

Hamm netted another catch of the day.

I said, "What is that?"

"That is a gizzard shad." Hamm did not lift the fish out of the netting. "These fish? They smell. They're very slimy, but their keels are sharp like a razor. They're used for cat food and fertilizer. Also very good crab bait."

Bob touched the shad and said, "He's greasy."

"There's a commercial market for them," Hamm said. He dumped the shad and went after the next one in the holding tank. There was a hole in his net, and this fish was small and wily. Hamm had to slide the net up the side of the tank to grasp the fish.

"Here we go," he said. It was a red-bellied bream—one of three, all different sizes. There was a difference in pigmentation from the small to the large. However, in all sizes, there is red on the belly and lines on the face.

"Red-bellies as opposed to bluegills? They're more in the riverine system." Hamm tossed the fish over the side of the boat and netted a tiny bream.

"That's my normal catch, right there," Bob said.

Hamm said, "This here…see that little red? It's called a redear sunfish." The fish leaped out of his hands and back into the tank. It took a while to get him back out. When fish are stunned, they are only immobile for a few minutes—at most. "This is a one-year old fish. He's small now, but he'll grow larger than the red-bellies—maybe two pounds."

I stared down at the sunfish no larger than the width of my hand and asked, "How do they survive, I wonder?"

"Cover," Hamm said. "And quantity. As opposed to humans. With our children we do a lot of parental care. Fish, by and large, have millions of progenies with the hope that a few make it to reproduce themselves."

Bob asked, "You just looking to see what species you have here?"

Hamm nodded and said, "We do what we call a community sample, where we're trying to find the species assemblage, and, like I said, build that trend over time. Do we need to stock fish, do we need to improve fish, what are their habitats? Species fish fill different niches within their environment. Flow and a little bit of change in vegetation, influence grouping. Speaking of which, I suspect any stumpknockers are twenty yards up the hill."

Later, when I looked them up, I found that stumpknockers are spotted sunfish with an affinity for submerged timber and slow-moving streams. The habitat of the Ocklawaha River was perfect for them.

Hamm turned back to the boat. "Let's run down the river a little more. I saw some gar pop up on the sonar." He turned the ignition, and the boat's engine began its gentle hum.

We passed banks wreathed with vegetation. "There's any number of plants," Hamm said. "I'm sure when Native Americans were using this river, they found plenty of things to eat. There's wild mustard, saw palmetto berries and hearts and the water hyacinth, to name just a few. Of course, you can catch fish to eat anywhere, all up and down the river."

The engine purred on the quiet river. We were all thinking of the reservoir. Hamm said, "In terms of fishing, a reservoir is a different system. The people that support keeping Rodman is because it's a functioning reservoir. I don't think anyone would disagree that it's one of the top three bass fisheries in Florida, nationally recognized. Fish are stable in an area like the reservoir, and they grow larger and fatter and produce more fish than one in a river. They produce more trophies."

Bob said, "We heard during the tournaments, most of the anglers leave the reservoir to catch their bass."

Hamm nodded, "The reservoir is connected to the St. Johns River. They'll go to Lake George; sometimes, they even go as far down as Lake Monroe out of Palatka. But, you know, fish move. The reservoir is consistently the top bass fishery. Same with Lake George." Lake George (also called Lake Welaka), a large and shallow lake, borders Putnam and Volusia Counties.

We did a few more dips and missed a huge tilapia, which seemed to recover from the electroshock more quickly than our nets could catch him. Then, we motored back to Ray Wayside Landing and thanked Ryan Hamm. It was pretty clear to us that he made the expedition for our educational benefit, since the high-water levels were not really conducive to electroshock fish sampling (although the inundated areas of species were quite interesting, and we may otherwise not have seen that).

This experience on the Ocklawaha gave us new information about the relationship of water to river flow, level, and fish communities—all important components in promoting ecological health along the Ocklawaha River.

2018

We forget that the water cycle and the life cycle are one.
—Jacques Cousteau

Bob and I decided that our book wouldn't be complete until we strayed off into one of the side creeks on the Ocklawaha River, where, instead of frenetically paddling to cover ground, we could instead sit quietly and wait for wildlife to emerge. Maybe we would dip our fishing poles in the water, and Bob could finally catch a fish.

We were on the road to Salt Springs by 6:00 a.m., kayaks tied to the rack on the car roof, heading for the boat launch off Highway 19. First, we stopped at the Square Meal Restaurant. On a glass pane on the door was the emblem "God First. Then Hunting. Then Fishing." As usual, everyone looked at us when we came in. The waitress served us coffee and asked, "Where you folks from?"

Bob said, "Near Orlando."

She replied, "So, what're you doing here?"

Through the window, I watched a man in a cowboy hat walk to his truck and take off, attached flags flying. Bob said, "We're fishing."

The waitress took out her pad for our order and gave us a friendly smile. "Ain't that cute. And don't they have fishing in Orlando?"

After a fine meal of eggs, grits, biscuits and sausage, we walked next door and sat down in some rocking chairs outside the Buck N Bass Sports Center. At exactly 8:00 a.m., the owner pulled up in a red Longhorn Ram truck.

First, he opened the door and let out his dog, an old mixed-breed lab that immediately came over and sniffed us. Then, he emerged and said, "You guys have the best seats in Salt Springs. Where you from?"

"Near Orlando," Bob said. "We'd like some nightcrawlers." Yesterday, Bob tried to teach me how to cast lines with lures, but I just wanted to sit there with a hook in the water. Bob said I needed worms to do that.

"It's shiner season," the owner said, unlocking the door.

The bait shop had heads of deer, elk and even impalas and water buffalo mounted on the walls. A stuffed bobcat was propped in the corner. There were also many pictures of anglers holding up humongous bass. An elderly guy in an undershirt and NASCAR baseball cap followed us in, trailing the smell of cigarette smoke.

"Lemme try out your Winchester," he said to the owner. The owner opened a safe behind the counter. When he reached to get the rifle, he revealed a pistol on his hip.

"You folks need a fishing license?" the owner asked, addressing me and Bob. We shook our heads, because we already had them. "Rodman dam's a good place to go for bass, bream, perch." He drummed his fingers on the counter. "You need bobbers?"

He sold us some nightcrawlers, and we got into Bob's old Nissan and drove to the boat launch just under Highway 19. There was a truck with symmetrical rusted holes in the side fender, its empty trailer parked on the sandy, rock-strewn lot. The weather was cloudy and looked like rain. Traffic was still slow, and we could hear the knocking sound of a woodpecker. A breeze ruffled the lily pads, and there were minnows in the marshy water.

The big tree that had been blocking the boat launch to the tributary when we met with Bob H. Lee wasn't exactly gone, but its branches were sawed off. We untied the ropes, unfastened the bungee hooks and pulled the yellow kayaks off the tie-down racks and down the short slope to the marshland. Bob always lets me get in first and pushes me off, and I was almost to the bridge by the time he caught up to me. It was the first time we'd kayaked on the river since our camping trip with Paddle Florida the previous December.

We paddled in our light canoes under the looming Highway 19 bridge to the sound of traffic. Two tall silver ladders reached from the wooden fenders to the top of the bridge. We passed, cutting left, then we were on the river, paddling upstream. Immediately, I struggled to keep the bow pointed ahead and dig in with my light paddle to go a tiny distance at a time.

Bob pointed to the right, and we cut into one of the side creeks. Matt Keene talks about these watery trails as braids that interweave with the river,

Bridge over Highway 19.

but to me, they were more like arteries leading away from and toward the heart of the current. It was shady, with flat, dark water, although there was a little current. There were still broken trees everywhere, but the paddling here—even upstream—was easier. The sound of traffic was already muffled. Instead, we heard the cry of a bird we'd heard before on the river—a bird that makes a kind of simian sound befitting a Tarzan movie. Maybe it was a pileated woodpecker.

The water didn't look too high, but Bob could put the length of his paddle in the water and not hit bottom.

We had never spent any time in these arteries—partly because we wanted to cover ground on the actual river, and partly because Mike O'Neal had warned us that we could get lost. But from where we sat, low in the water with a clear view ahead, this was no different from the paddling we had done from our own dock in Crystal River. Or perhaps we were not so inexperienced anymore, not so prone to navigational errors. Bob had even remembered to bring a compass.

A white ibis flew overhead and came to rest on a high tree branch. When we caught up, it flew on ahead. This went on for a while, us

Anhinga drying its wings on a tree snag on the Ocklawaha.

following the bird (or vice versa). Finally, we came to rest on top of a fallen limb with air plants all over it. Bob opened the paper container of nightcrawlers and peered inside: "These guys are lively."

Rather than pass worms back and forth, I handed him my fishing pole, and he baited my line and cast it. He cast his bass lure, a reddish worm, a few times. After fifteen minutes without a bite, we pressed on.

Instead of the bridge, cypress trees towered above us, banded by knobby cypress knees. I paddled past fallen trees with their huge, chunky, sod-covered roots upended toward the sky. The white bird flew on ahead. I saw more white ibises in the marshland, far back, as far as the eye could see.

The biggest monarch butterfly I ever saw fluttered by, and I remembered the butterfly that landed on my baseball cap during our motorboat ride upstream with Bob H. Lee in October. We passed an anhinga perched in a tree, holding its wings aloft.

"If there's birds, there must be fish," I said.

We launched the kayaks on a fallen log, but every line we cast got tangled in the trees. Then, the monofilament crossed the deck of the kayaks and got stuck in the stern until we were pretty much hopelessly mired and wrapped up in our own fishing lines.

Part of the problem was that every time we cast, the kayak shifted. "Never fish from a kayak," I said, trying to disentangle myself. I lost my worm and gave up. We sorted out the lines and started paddling again. A little way upstream, the water was roiling as bass went after shiners. We cast our lines again, and mine caught on an underwater branch and broke off as my kayak spun around fecklessly.

"Let's forget fishing and have fun on the river," I said, starting to drift down the creek, just as Bob simultaneously said, "I've got a bite!" We both whooped, and I spun my kayak around and began paddling toward him. Bob pulled a footlong black bass out of the water and held it up.

Bob catches a black bass on the Ocklawaha side creek. *Elizabeth Randall.*

I forgot to paddle for a second and began drifting downstream. Then, I dug the paddle into the water and turned around, holding my phone aloft to get some fine pictures of Bob's back, the hull of the kayak, and—finally—one of him holding the bass above the bow of the yellow kayak.

White bird in
the distance.

Then, he released it—although it wasn't quite as easy as that. The hook was dug in deep, and by the time he got it out, we were both afraid the bass was dead. Bob put it back in the water and said, "Oh no." We looked. The fish was on its side and remained motionless…for a few seconds. Then, it took off, a fleeting shadow in the dark water.

We reeled in our lines and paddled as far as we could down the artery of dark, smooth water. A hawk crossed our path, flying low, laden with a big frog clutched in its talons. We paddled until a mass of fallen trees laid across the length of the stream stopped us. We squinted into sunbeams cast through gaps in the trees, each one swarming with dandelion wisps.

A flock of ibises flew back and forth or perched in the trees. Then, the sun broke through and lit up the changing colors of the leaves. Turtles started to come out in pairs and trios on branches sticking out of the water, and a young gator sunned itself on a log. Ever vigilant, the critters slid into the water at the slightest sound as though they were being wiped from the branches

White heron and ibis perch on the Ocklawaha River.

by an unseen hand. The wild surroundings animated me. I remembered my childhood, returning home carrying things that interested me: a rock, a feather, an oddly colored leaf.

And I thought back to the kayaking trip Bob and I took in December, when we were on the river all day long for days at a time. I thought about

Alligator in side creek.

how tired I was and how I strained to dig the heavy paddle in and out of the water, to create a rhythm that was sustainable. Back and forth, back and forth. It was a little like childbirth. Both experiences were long-term and required endurance. After childbirth, parents bask in the aura of the new life they've created. Paddling a length of the river—feeling the rush of the wind, the sound of the water, the sensation of sunshine on skin—also creates an aura of a new life, an inner life in the heart of nature, which is, at once, the center of all creation.

The clouds above us were moving fast, but this time, we were in no hurry. We let the current slowly carry us back to the river.

BIBLIOGRAPHY

Abbott, Elizabeth A. "Twenty Springs of the Oklawaha. An Occasional Paper prepared for the Florida Defenders of the Environment, Inc." University of Florida Department of Geology, 1971.

Adams, Donnie. Personal interview by Elizabeth Randall. March 10, 2018.

Alvarez, Lizette. "Florida Struggles to Overcome Threats to Freshwater Springs." *New York Times*, June 22, 2012.

Alvers, Nancy, and Janice Machaffrey Smith. *Our Place in Time: A Chronology of Putnam County*. Palatka, FL: Palatka Printing Company, 1995.

Barnett, Cynthia. *Mirage: Florida and the Vanishing Water of the Eastern U.S.* Ann Arbor: University of Michigan Press, 2007.

Barton, Greg. Phone interview by Elizabeth Randall. November 29, 2017.

Bass, Jack. Personal interview by Elizabeth Randall. September 4, 2017.

Beaton, Larry. "Steamboats of the St. Johns and Ocklawaha Rivers." Lecture presented at a meeting of the Historical Society of Orange Park at T.C. Miller Community Center, Orange Park, FL, October 16, 2017.

Bi, Xiang, Tatiana Borisova, Alan Hodges, and Stephen Holland. "Economic Importance and Public Preferences for Water Resource Management of the Ocklawaha River." Department of Tourism, Recreation, and Sport Management, University of Florida, November 11, 2017.

Bloomfield, Max. *Bloomfield's Illustrated Historical Guide, Embracing an Account of the Antiquities of St. Augustine, Florida (with Map). To Which is Added a Condensed Guide of the St. Johns, Ocklawaha, Halifax, and Indian Rivers*. St. Augustine, FL: 1892.

"Boat Works Owner Hatten Howard Dies." *Daytona Beach Sunday News-Journal*, November 11, 1975.

Boning, Charles R. "Ocklawaha River." In *Florida's Rivers*. Sarasota, FL: Pineapple Press, 2007.

Boyer, Willet A., III. "The Acuera Of the Ocklawaha River Valley: Keepers of Time in the Land of the Waters." PhD diss., University of Florida, 2010.

Brooks, Paul. "Oklawaha: The Sweetest Water-Lane in the World." *Audubon Magazine*, July 1970.

————. "Time Capsule: Canal Threatens Florida's Ocklawaha River." *Audubon Magazine*, July 1970.

Bryan, Judith, C. "Environmental Studies Concerning Four Alternatives for Rodman Reservoir and the Lower Ocklawaha River." St. Johns River Water Management District, Palatka, FL, 1994.

Callan, Kevin. "Dealing with Strainers & Sweepers." Paddling.com. https://paddling.com/learn/dealing-with-strainers-sweepers/.

Cardenas, Danae. *Refuge of the Sacred and Profane: Trail through the Past and Present of the Cross Florida Greenway*. Master's degree research project, University of Florida, 2014.

Carr, Marjorie H. "The Ocklawaha River Wilderness." *Florida Naturalist*, August 1965.

Carson, Rachel. *Silent Spring*. New York: Houghton Mifflin Harcourt, 1962.

Chadwick, Karen. "History of the Ocklawaha River." Lecture presented at Ocklawaha Canoe Outpost and Resort, Fort McCoy, FL, December 3, 2017.

Chrisman, Thomas. Email message to author ("Re: Referred by Jim Gross; Dams regulate downstream flow"), January 8, 2018.

Deal, Scott. "Hooked on Florida Fishing? End Outdated Federal Rules." *Orlando Sentinel*, May 7, 2018.

Dearen, Jason. "Herpes B Risk: State Wants to Remove Silver River Monkeys." *Ocala Star Banner*, January 10, 2018.

Dowda, Robert B. *The History of Palatka and Putnam County*. Palatka, FL: Palatka South Historic District, 1939.

"Down to the Bone: Diver Mike Stallings Examines a Part of a Mastodon's Scapula." *Palatka Daily News*, October 17, 2017.

Ericson, Edward, Jr. "The Green Swamp." *Orlando Weekly*, January 6, 2000.

"FDE Joins Kaster and Little in Lawsuit Against Forest Service to Free Ocklawaha." *The Monitor* (newsletter of Florida Defenders of the Environment), February 2018.

Florida Defenders of the Environment, Inc., coordinators Marjorie H. Carr, John H. Kaufman and Jeffery Bielling, contributor John H. Hankinson Jr. "Restoring the Ocklawaha River Ecosystem." August 1989.

Florida Fish and Wildlife Conservation Commission. "Rodman Reservoir Historical Perspective." April 2015.

Florida Natural Resources Leadership Institute. "Rodman Reservoir/ Ocklawaha River," a report by FNRLI Fellows of Class VII, Session VI, August 16–18, 2007.

Gallant, Gene. "River Boats Competed With Each Other for Business on Ocklawaha, St. Johns." *Ocala Star-Banner*, April 17, 1963.

Gross, Jim. Email message to author ("Re: Questions Ocklawaha River"), October 25, 2017.

———. "Florida Headed for Water Wars." *Gainesville Sun*, April 7, 2017.

———. Phone interview by Elizabeth Randall. October 17, 2017.

Hafner, E.R. "County Commissioners' View of the Noxious Weed Problem." State Association of County Commissioners, 1968.

Hamm, Ryan. Phone interview by Elizabeth Randall. January 29, 2018.

Henrickson, John. "Technical Publication SJ2016-1 Effects on Lower St. Johns River Nutrient Supply and TMDL Target Compliance from the Restoration of a Free-Flowing Ocklawaha River." Palatka, FL: St. Johns River Water Management District, 2016.

Hensley, Donald R., Jr. "The Ocklawaha Valley Railroad and the Rodman Lumber Company." Taplines (blog). http://taplines.net/OV/OV.html.

Howard, Brian Clark. "River Revives After Largest Dam Removal in U.S. History." *National Geographic*, June 2, 2016.

Howard, Hatten J. "Sternwheeling on Jungle Rivers." *Motorboating*, January 1942.

Jackson, Kristina. "Evaluate Ocklawaha Restoration Permits," *Gainesville Sun*, July 10, 1999.

Johnson, Clifton. *The Stately St. Johns and the Beautiful Ocklawaha Highways and Byways of Florida.* New York: Macmillan Company, 1918.

Karst Environmental Services, Inc. (prepared for St. Johns Water Management District). "Discharge Measurement: Blue Spring, Rodman Reservoir/Ocklawaha River, Marion County, Florida." Palatka, FL: September 27, 2007.

Keene, Matt. Email message to author ("Re: Fwd: Book Proposal on the Ocklawaha River"), January 31, 2018.

Keene, Matt, dir. *Lost Springs.* Film screening at the Museum of Contemporary Art (MOCA), Jacksonville, FL, September 24, 2017.

————. *River be Dammed: The Kirkpatrick Dam's Lasting Uncertainty.*

Lanier, Sidney. *FLORIDA: Its Scenery, Climate, and History.* Bicentennial Commission of Florida, 1973.

Lee, Bob H. *Backcountry Lawman: True Stories from a Florida Game Warden.* Gainesville: University Press of Florida, 2015.

————. Personal interview by Elizabeth Randall, October 8, 2017.

Lee, Henry. *The Tourist's Guide of Florida and the Winter Resorts of the South… Containing Descriptions of Washington, Norfolk, Wilmington…Lists of Hotels, Prominent Resorts and How to Reach Them.* New York: Liberty Print, 1886.

Leitner, Annabelle. "Our Towns: Grahamville Once Thrived on the Banks of the Ocklawaha River." *Ocala Star-Banner,* November 27, 2017.

Macdonald, Margaret F. (Peggy). *Marjorie Harris Carr: Defender of Florida's Environment.* Gainesville: University Press of Florida, 2014.

————. "Our Lady of the Rivers: Marjorie Harris Carr, Science, Gender and Political Activism." PhD diss., University of Florida, Gainesville, 2010.

Michaels, Brian E. *The River Flows North: A History of Putnam County, Florida.* Palatka, FL: Fine Books Division, Taylor Publishing Company, 1986.

Miller, James, N. "Rape on the Ocklawaha." *Reader's Digest,* January 1970.

Mitchell, C. Bradford. *Paddle-Wheel Inboard.* N.p.: Reprints in Marine History from the Steamboat Historical Society of America, Literary Licensing LLC, 1983

Moore, Clarence B. "Certain Sand Mounds of the Ocklawaha River, Florida." Philadelphia, PA: Journal of the Academy of Natural Sciences of Philadelphia, 1893.

Mueller, Edward A. *Along the St. Johns and Ocklawaha Rivers.* Charleston, SC: Arcadia Publishing, 1999.

————. *Ocklawaha River Steamboats.* DeLeon Springs, FL: E.O. Painter Printing Company, 1983.

Noll, Steven. "Steamboats, Cypress, & Tourism: An Ecological History of the Ocklawaha Valley in the Late Nineteenth Century." *Florida Historical Quarterly,* Summer 2004.

Noll, Steven, and David Tegeder. *Ditch of Dreams: The Cross-Florida Barge Canal and the Struggle for Florida's Future.* Gainesville: University Press of Florida, 2015.

Nosca, Paul, and Erika Ritter. "Ocklawaha River, Florida, A 'Braided-Stream' with Auxiliary or Secondary Channels (a.k.a. Side-Creeks): An Information, Opinion and Photos Report Compiled by 'Ocklawahaman' Paul Nosca." February 6, 2013.

"Ocklawaha River Listening Sessions." Discussion at meeting of Florida Defenders of the Environment, Palatka, FL, October 24, 2017.

Ott, Eloise Robinson, and Louis Hickman Chazal. *Ocali Country, Kingdom of the Sun: A History of Marion County, Florida*. Ocala, FL: Marion Publishers, 1986.

Paddle Florida, Inc. Ocklawaha Odyssey itinerary, Gainesville, FL, 2017.

Powers, Ormund. "Rascally Oscar the River Gator Stops a Steamboat and Hitches a Ride." *Orlando Sentinel Lake Reflections*, December 18, 1996.

Prial, Francis P. *The Motor Boat: Devoted to All Types of Power Craft*, vol. 6. New York: Motor Boat Publishing Co., 1909 (digitized February 26, 2011).

Rawlings, Marjorie Kinnan. *Cross Creek*. New York: Charles Scribner's Sons, 1942.

————. *South Moon Under*. New York: Bantam Books, 1945.

Rohrer, Gray. "Scott's Campaign Ads Draw Criticism." *Orlando Sentinel*, July 15, 2018.

Sargent, Bill. "Florida Reservoir Yields Another 14-Pound Bass." *Florida Today*, February 1, 2015.

"The Silver Ocklawaha Blueway." *The Monitor*, February 2018.

Smith, Kent. "The Effects of Proposed Restoration of the Ocklawaha River in the Vicinity of the Rodman Basin on Manatee and Manatee Habitat." Report for the Office of Greenways and Trails, Division of Marine Resources, Bureau of Protected Species Management, Florida Department of Environmental Protection. Tallahassee, FL, July 1997.

Spear, Kevin. "State Debate over Kayak, Canoe Fees Persists." *Orlando Sentinel*, November 25, 2017.

————. "Water Levels Create Paradise for Snail Kites and Manatees." *Orlando Sentinel*, July 7, 2018.

Stallings, Michael. Personal interview by Elizabeth Randall, November 3, 2017.

State of Florida Department of Environmental Protection Division of Recreation and Parks. "Marjorie Harris Carr Cross Florida Greenway State Recreation and Conservation Area Unit Management Plan (2017–2027)."

Stepzinski, Teresa. "Putnam County Unites to Save Rodman Dam." *St. Augustine Record*, January 24, 2015.

St. Johns River Water Management District. "Ocklawaha River Water Allocation Study." 2005.

————. "Submerged Springs Site Documentation." August and September 2007.

"Sunday Editorial: A Deeper Harbor, a Stronger Jacksonville." *Florida Times-Union*, August 11, 2017.

Talbot, A.R., M.H. Shiaw, J.S. Huang, S.F. Yang, T.S. Goo, S.H. Wang, C.L. Chen and T.R. Sanford. "Acute Poisoning with a Glyphosate-Surfactant Herbicide ('Roundup'): A Review of 93 Cases." *Human & Experimental Toxicology*, January 1991.

Tarter, Steve. "Attack of the Superweeds." *Journal Star* (Peoria, IL), April 7, 2009.

University of Florida Department of Fisheries and Aquatic Sciences. "Relationship Between River Surface Level and Fish Assemblage in the Ocklawaha River, Florida." Gainesville: Florida Fish and Wildlife Conservation Commission, 1983–1994.

URS Corporation Southern (for the Florida Department of Environmental Protection). "Kirkpatrick Dam and Spillway Condition Assessment." July 2015.

U.S. Forest Service. "For the Ocklawaha River Restoration Project, Marion and Putnam Counties: Environmental Impact Statement." 2001.

"Wildlife Study by Florida Game & Fresh Water Fish Commission." Prepared for the U.S. Army Corps of Engineers, Jacksonville District. 1976.

Wilson, Edward O. *The Future of Life*. New York: Vintage Press, 2003.

ABOUT THE AUTHOR AND PHOTOGRAPHER

Jack Bass.

Bob and Elizabeth Randall are a husband-and-wife photojournalist team who have been creating books about local Florida history for almost a decade. Bob is a small-business owner and website master for car-stereo repair. He is also a professional photographer whose pictures have been nationally published and prominently displayed in local art festivals. Elizabeth is a high school English teacher and a widely published freelance writer. To get her stories, she has interviewed prisoners on death row, traipsed through haunted houses and camped in humid tents. She has also presented guest lectures at book conferences and won first- and second-place writing awards from the Florida Authors and Publishers Association and the Royal Palm Literary Society. Bob and Elizabeth live in Lake Mary, Florida. Their previous credits include *The Floating Teacher: A Guide to Surviving and Thriving* (Maupin House), *Haunted St. Augustine and St. Johns County* (The History Press), *Women in White: The Haunting of Northeast Florida* (Schiffer Publishing) and *Murder in St. Augustine: The Mysterious Death of Athalia Ponsell Lindsley* (The History Press).